AF576908

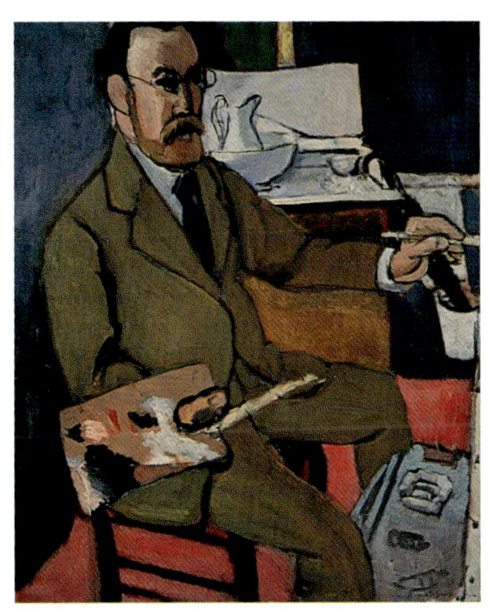

The moment I had this box of colors in my hands,
I had the feeling that my life was there.

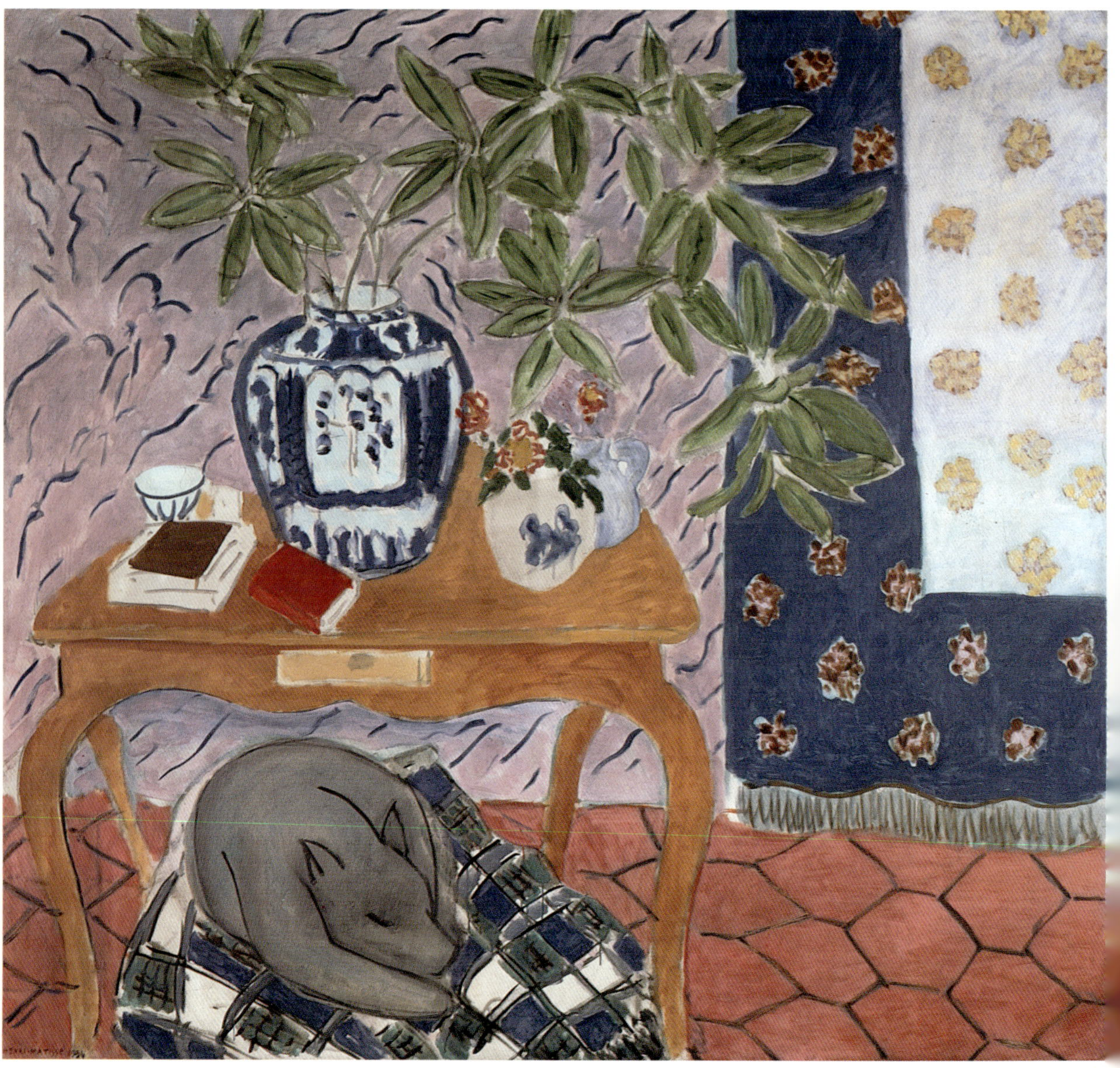

MATISSE
the artist speaks

EDITED BY GENEVIEVE MORGAN

CollinsPublishersSanFrancisco
A Division of HarperCollins*Publishers*

First published in USA 1996 by
Collins Publishers San Francisco
1160 Battery Street, San Francisco, CA 94111

HarperCollins Web Site: http://www.harpercollins.com

Design: Kari Perin
Design and Production Coordination: Kristen Wurz

Library of Congress Cataloging-in-Publication Data
Matisse, Henri, 1869–1954.
Matisse, the artist speaks / edited by Genevieve Morgan.
p. cm.
Includes index.
ISBN 0-00-255458-5
1. Matisse, Henri, 1869–1954--Aesthetics.
2. Painting--Psychology. I. Morgan, Genevieve. II. Title.
ND553.M37A2 1996
759.4--dc20 95-25200
CIP

Printed in China
10 9 8 7 6 5 4 3 2 1

The editor gratefully acknowledges the following sources:

Barr, Alfred H., Jr. *Matisse: His Art and His Public.* (New York: The Museum of Modern Art). Copyright 1951.

Elderfield, John. *Henri Matisse: A Retrospective.* (New York: The Museum of Modern Art). Copyright 1992.

Elderfield, John. *Matisse: In the Collection of The Museum of Modern Art.* (New York: The Museum of Modern Art). Copyright 1978.

Flam. Jack, ed.: *Matisse on Art.* (New York: Phaidon). Copyright 1973.

Flam, Jack. *Matisse: The Man and His Art, 1869-1918.* (Ithaca, NY: Cornell University Press). Copyright 1986.

Gilot, Françoise. *Matisse and Picasso: A Friendship in Art.* (New York: Doubleday). Copyright 1990.

Matisse, Henri. *Jazz.* (New York: George Braziller) English edition copyright 1983, estate of Henri Matisse.

Schneider, Pierre. *Matisse* (New York: Rizzoli). Copyright 1984.

Exhibition catalog. *Henri Matisse.* Copyright 1973 Acquavella Galleries.

Exhibition catalog. *Matisse: 1869-1954.* A retrospective exhibition at the Hayward Gallery. Copyright 1968 The Arts Council of Great Britain.

In addition, the editor wishes to thank Liz Weissberg at Artists Rights Society; Jenny Barry, Maura Carey Damacion, Katie Morris, Kari Perin, Carole Vandermeyde and Kristen Wurz at Collins Publishers; each of the institutions and their personnel who graciously gave their time and permission to reproduce images from their collection; and finally, a special thanks to the estate of Henri Matisse for granting permission to use the artist's works and writing.

INTRODUCTION

Henri Matisse is famous for his instruction to students, "You want to paint? First of all you must cut off your tongue because your decision takes away from you the right to express yourself with anything but your brush." Throughout his lifetime (1869-1954), Matisse strove to present his emotions clearly, without muddying their purity with the complexity of detail or personal context. He was accustomed to situating written phrases alongside images; the words accompanied the image, creating structure and balance, a "purely visual" effect. As he states in his book *Jazz,* the writing helps "just as asters help in the composition of a bouquet of more important flowers." In seeing the finished juxtaposition of words and images in this book, it occurred to me that Matisse might have preferred his words to be splashed across the page, handwritten and not typeset beside the images, but nonetheless, he might be pleased with the vigorous impact the combination has on the eye. Whether he would have actually read these words or not is anyone's guess. For Matisse, literal meaning was superfluous, even if he was the source; what mattered most was immediate, luxurious sensation and, ultimately, expression.

And what expression! Pure energy, drenching color, radical composition, interiors so lush and voluptuous you feel as if you could scoop them up in a spoon. His friend Françoise Gilot writes in her memoirs: "No one can resist a still life by Matisse. They are so delectable; it is like a frenzy, you absorb them, you eat them up—you don't look at them, you lick them with your eyes, and they taste of ginger and cardamom, of orange blossoms and turmeric, they assuage an inexhaustible hunger and quench a spiritual thirst." At first, not everyone enjoyed the bounty of Matisse's creations. Dubbed the Fauves (or "Savages"), he and his colleagues were roundly criticized at the 1905 Salon d'Automne for their crude, bordering on "ugly", sense of color. It was not long, however, before Matisse was recognized for his revolutionary work. Here was something the world had *really* never seen before.

There is always some minor trepidation when collecting a small cross-section of an artist's work, especially when that artist is one of the greatest painters of the twentieth century—the founding father of modern art. Matisse's work is admired and loved on all continents, and a great deal of the images and perhaps even some of the phrases presented here will be familiar. His *oeuvre* is remarkable not only for its extraordinary quality but for its sheer quantity. In unstoppable pursuit of new venues in which he could *create* feeling, Matisse experimented in several mediums in addition to painting, including drawing, lithograph, etching, woodcut, collage, and writing. Matisse crafted several notebooks and was able to crystallize his ideas about art and process, recording them in several interviews, radio broadcasts, and introductions to his books. A social, if often bed-ridden, conversant, Matisse's fellow painters, students, friends, and writers had ample opportunity to share his ideas, passions, and clarity. Choice excerpts from much of this material appear here.

Capturing the essence of Matisse is a tricky business, and one that he would not advise. Instead, I think that he would ask that one not think, upon viewing his art, but *react* with pure instinct and open senses. As Pablo Picasso, a friend and great admirer, often said, "All things considered, there is only Matisse."

—*Genevieve Morgan*

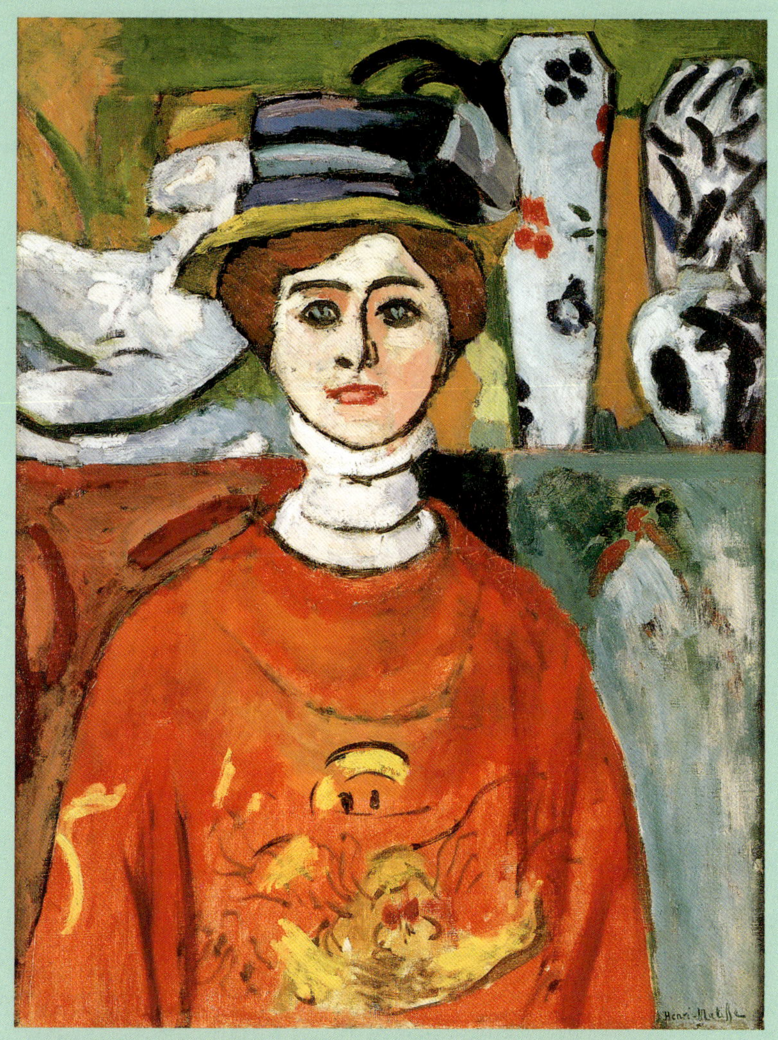
Henri-Matisse

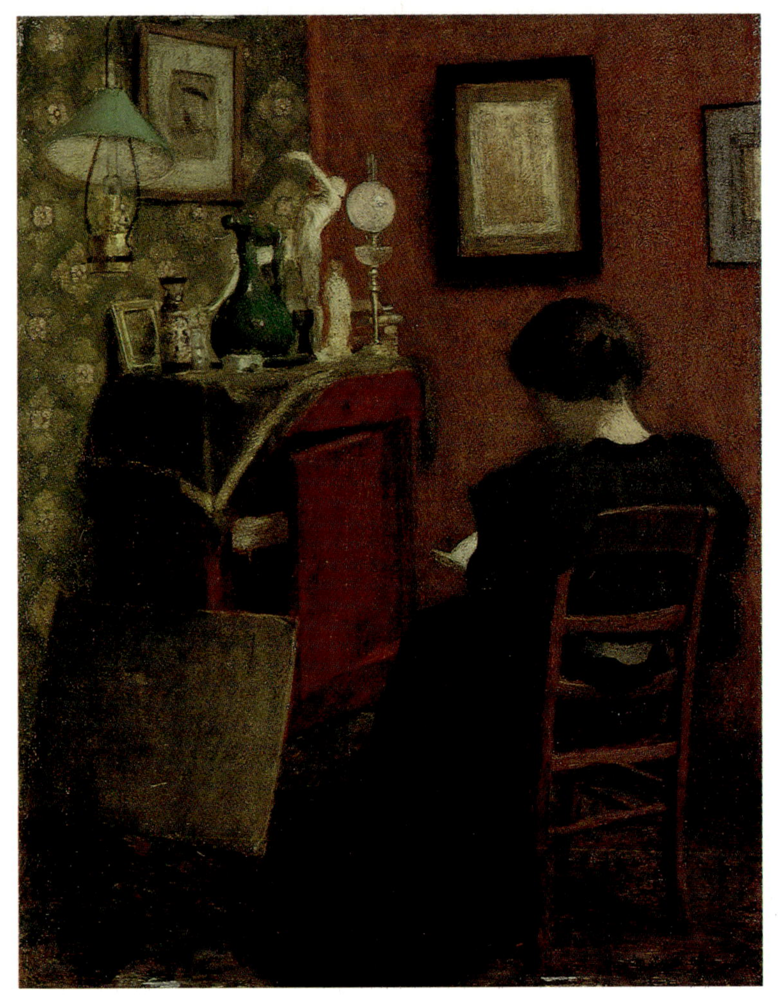

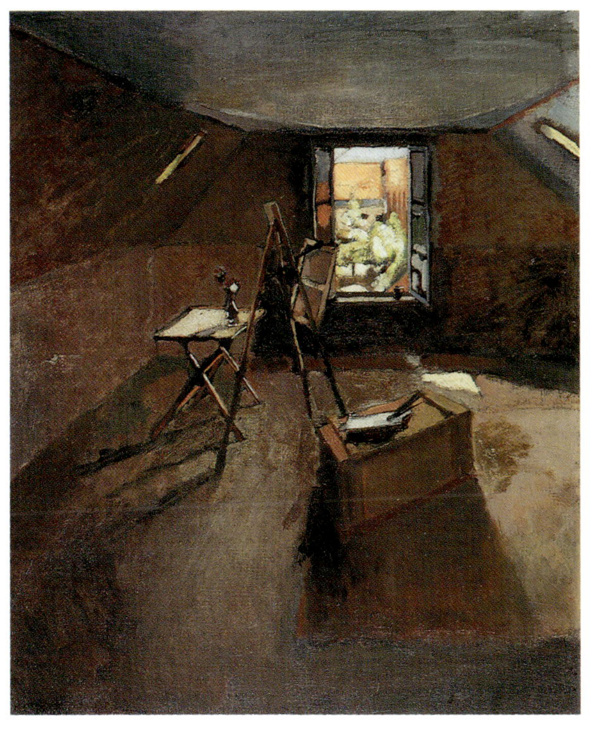

When I started to paint, I felt transported into a kind of paradise. . . .
In everyday life, I was usually bored and vexed by the things
that people were always telling me I must do. Starting to paint,
I felt gloriously free, quiet, and alone.

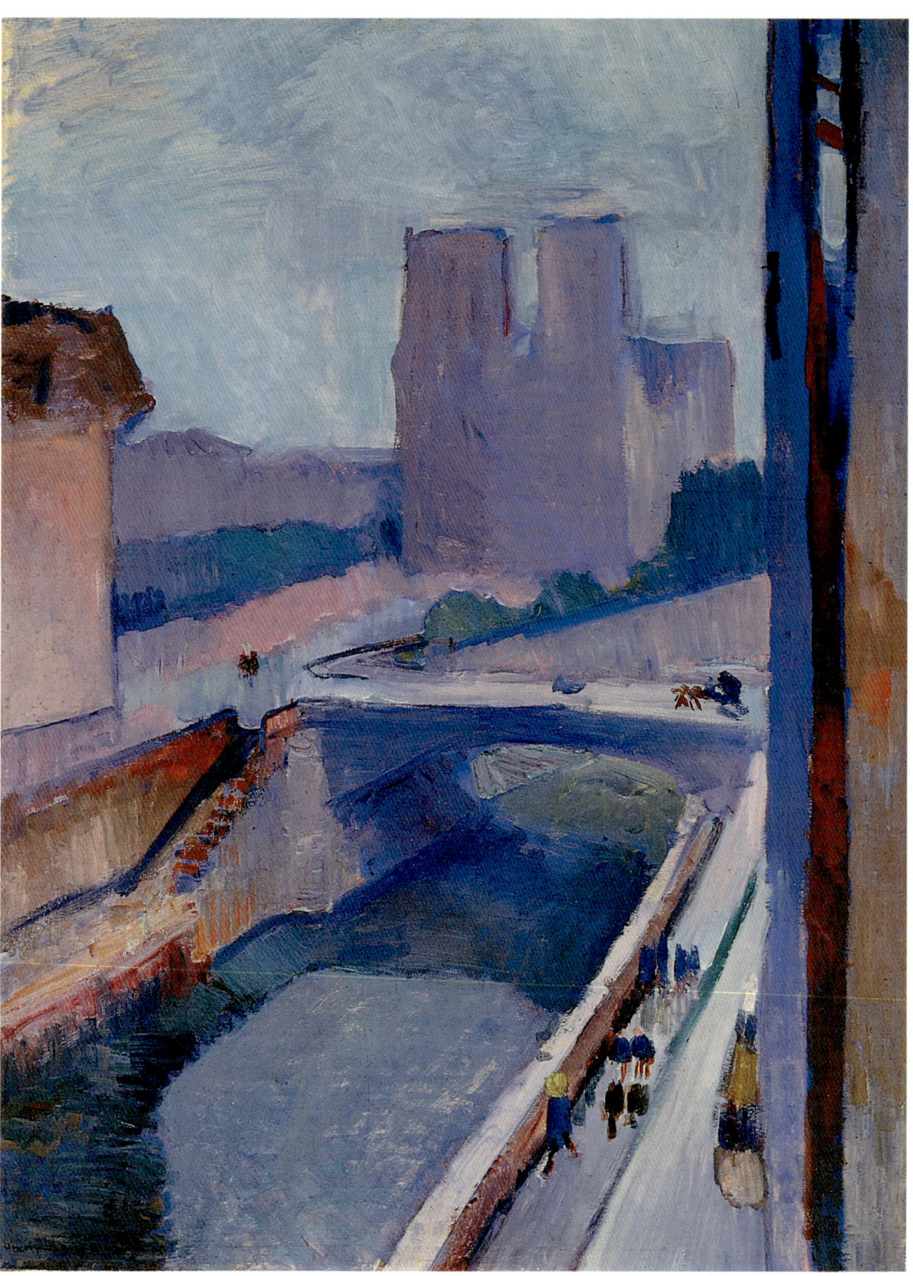

A rapid rendering
of a landscape represents
only one moment
of its appearance.
I prefer, by insisting
upon its essentials,
to discover its
more enduring character...

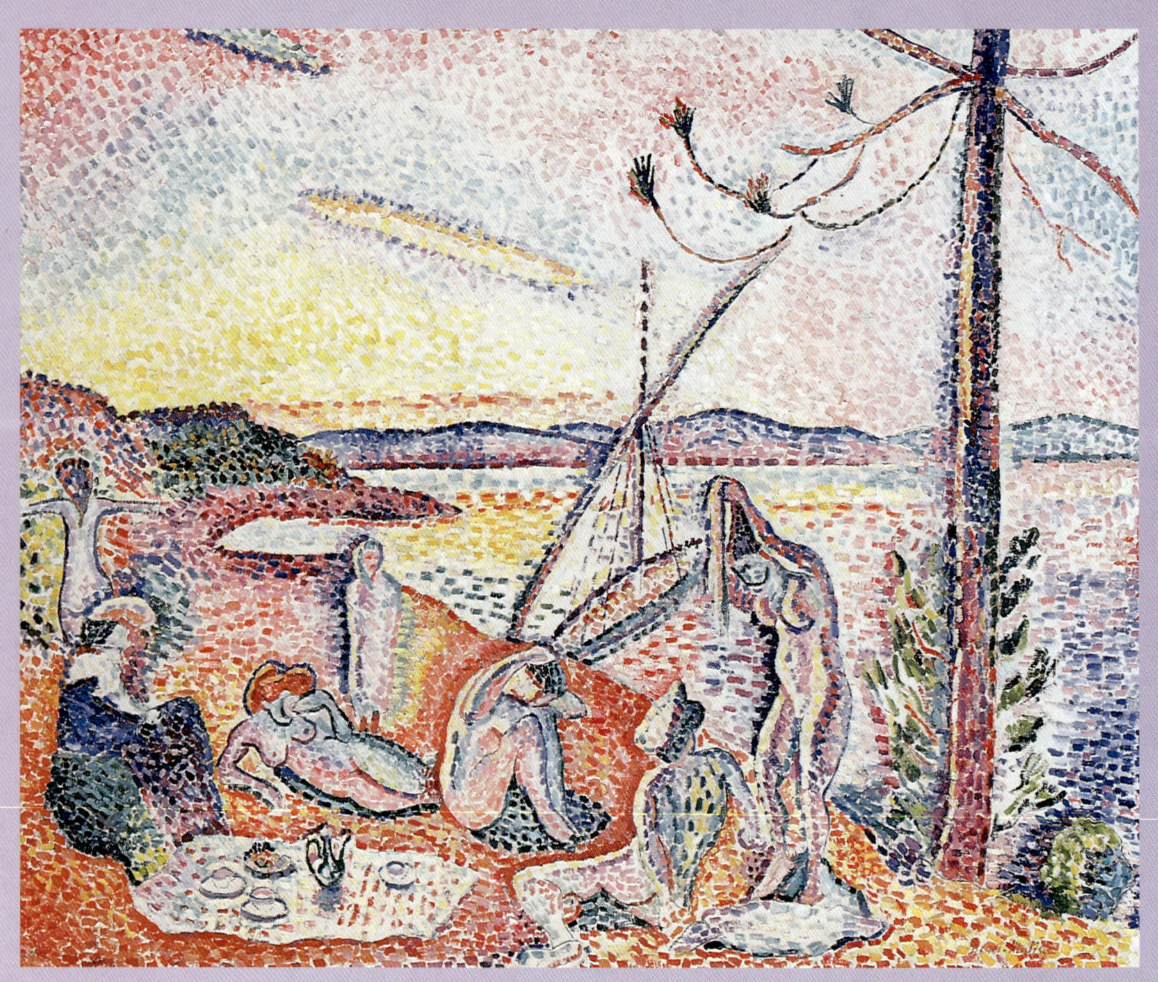

We were at the time like children in the face of nature and we let our temperaments speak.

The man who has

meditated on himself for

a certain length of time

comes back to life sensing

the position he can occupy.

Then he can act effectively.

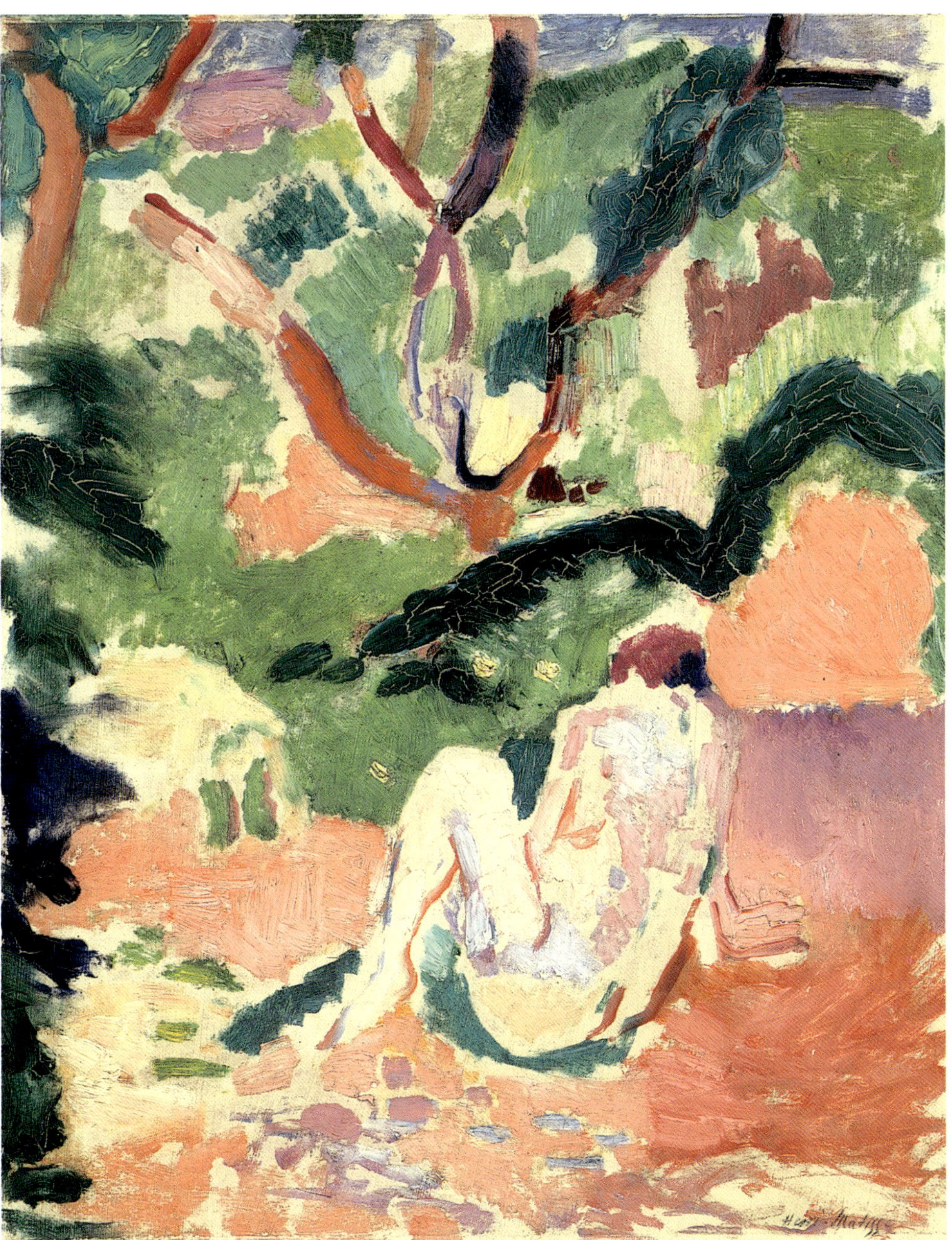
Henri-Matisse

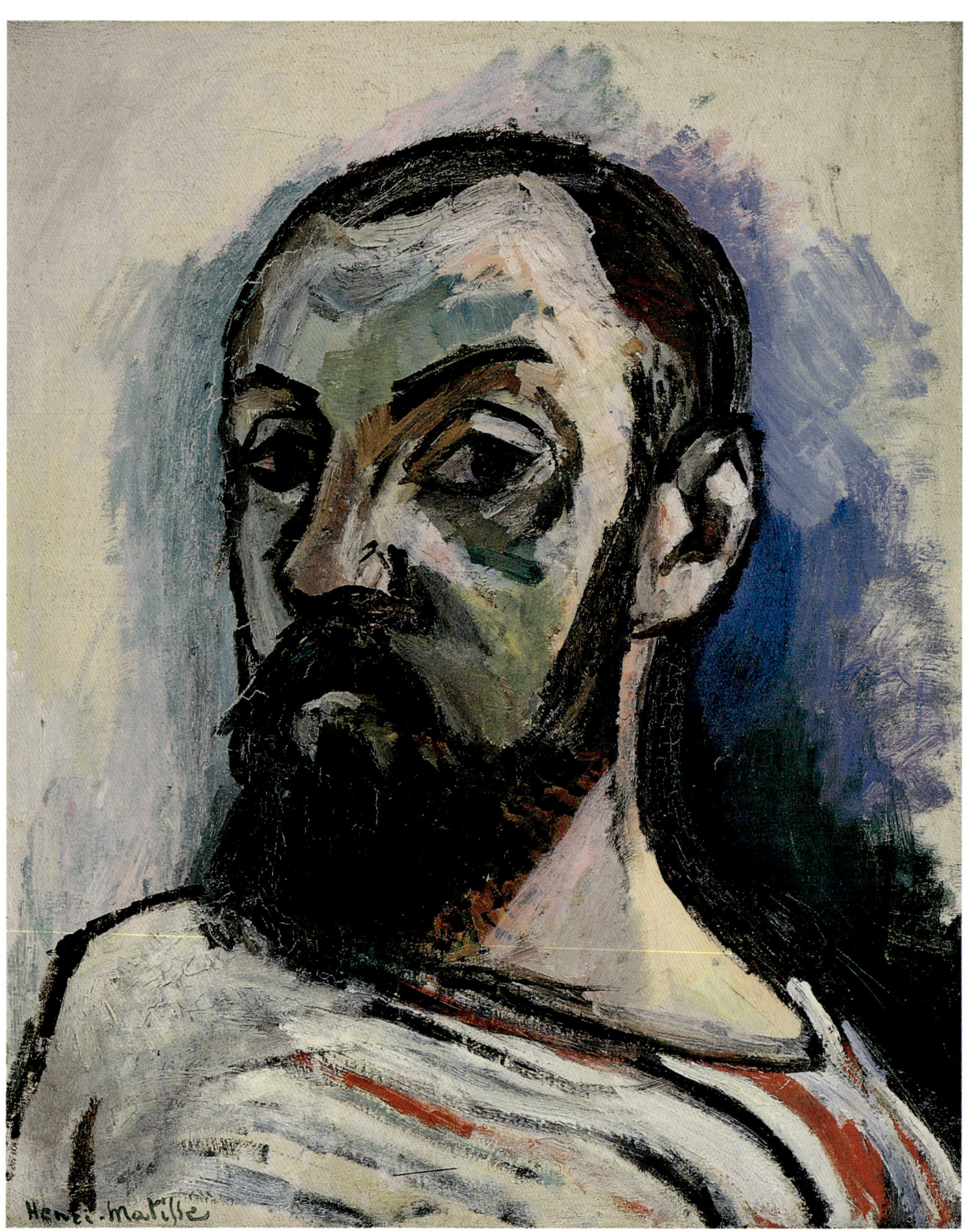
Henri-Matisse

The truly original artist invents his own signs. . . .
The importance of an artist is to be measured by
the number of new signs he has introduced
into the language of art.

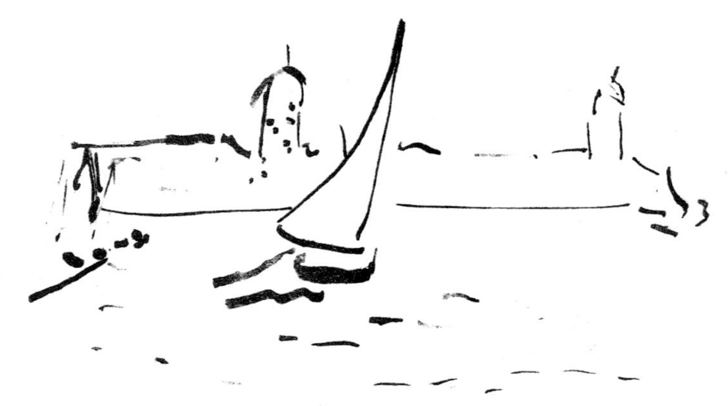

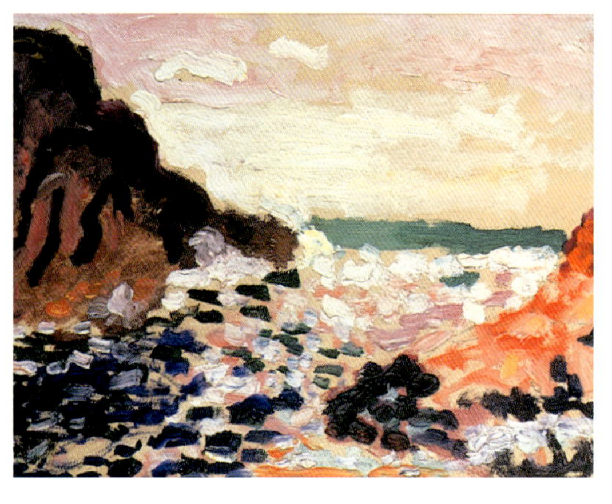

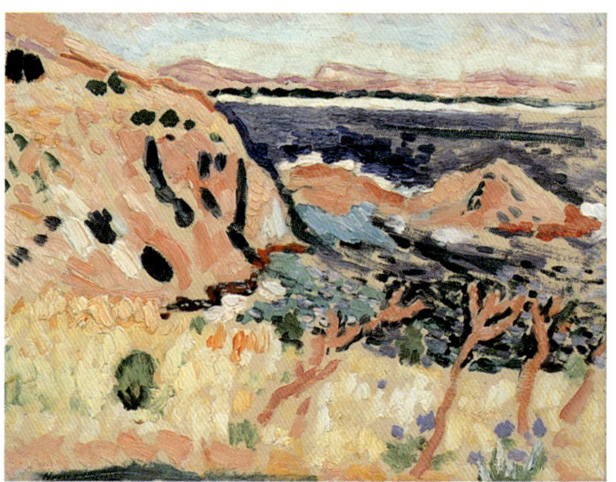

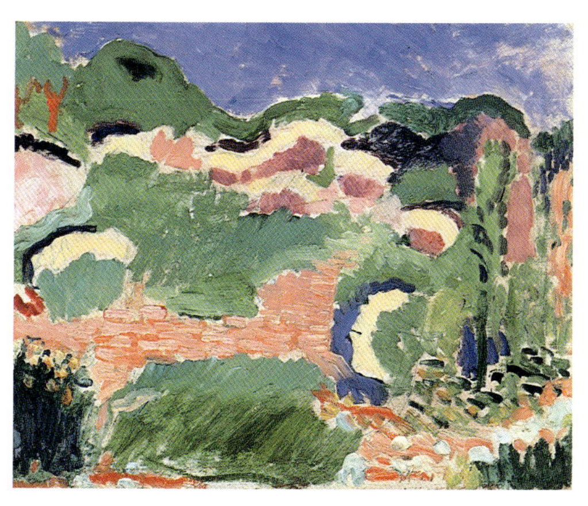

I cannot copy nature
in a servile way;
I must interpret nature
and submit it to
the spirit of the picture.

All things have their decided physical character . . .

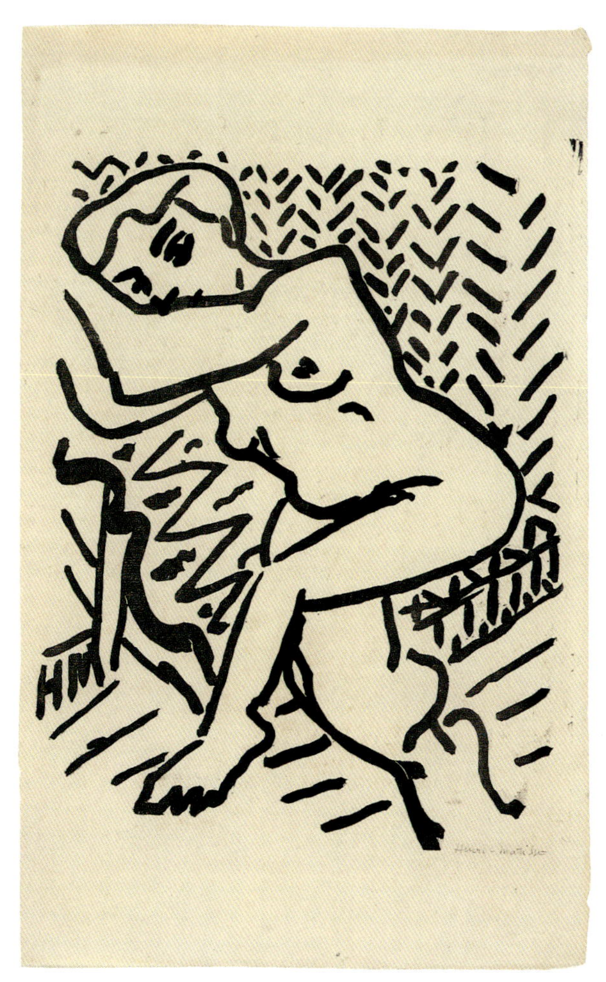

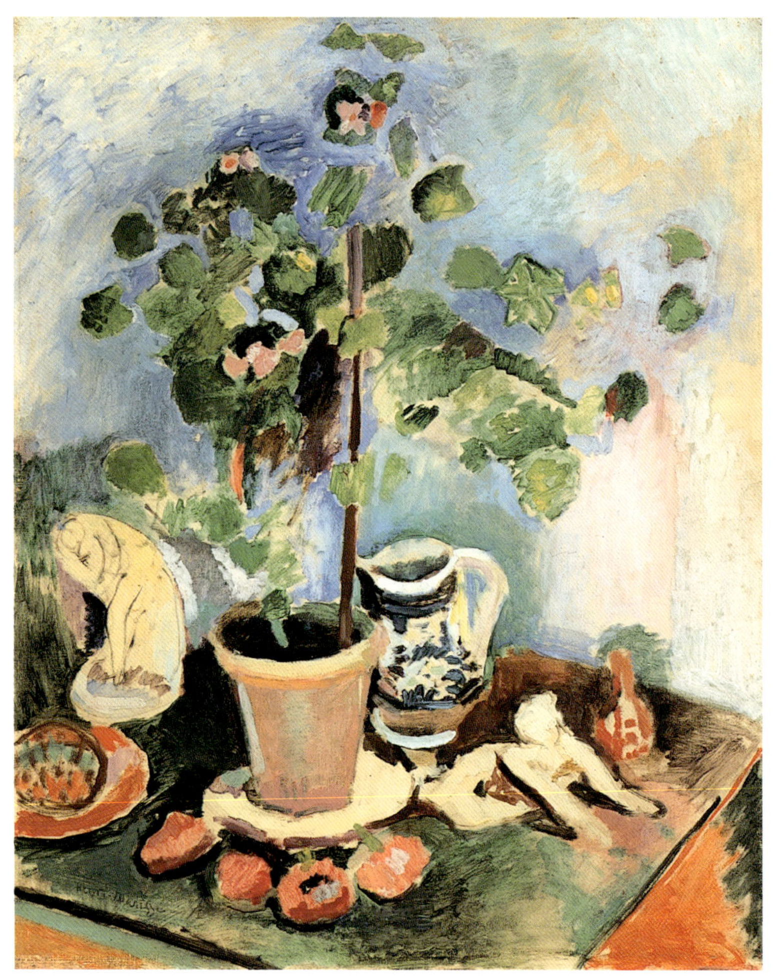

I found myself or my artistic personality
by looking over my earlier works.
They rarely deceive.
There I found something
that was always the same and
which at first glance
I thought to be monotonous repetition.
It was the mark of my personality,
which appeared the same no matter
what different states of mind
I happened to have passed through.

Nature excites the imagination to representation.

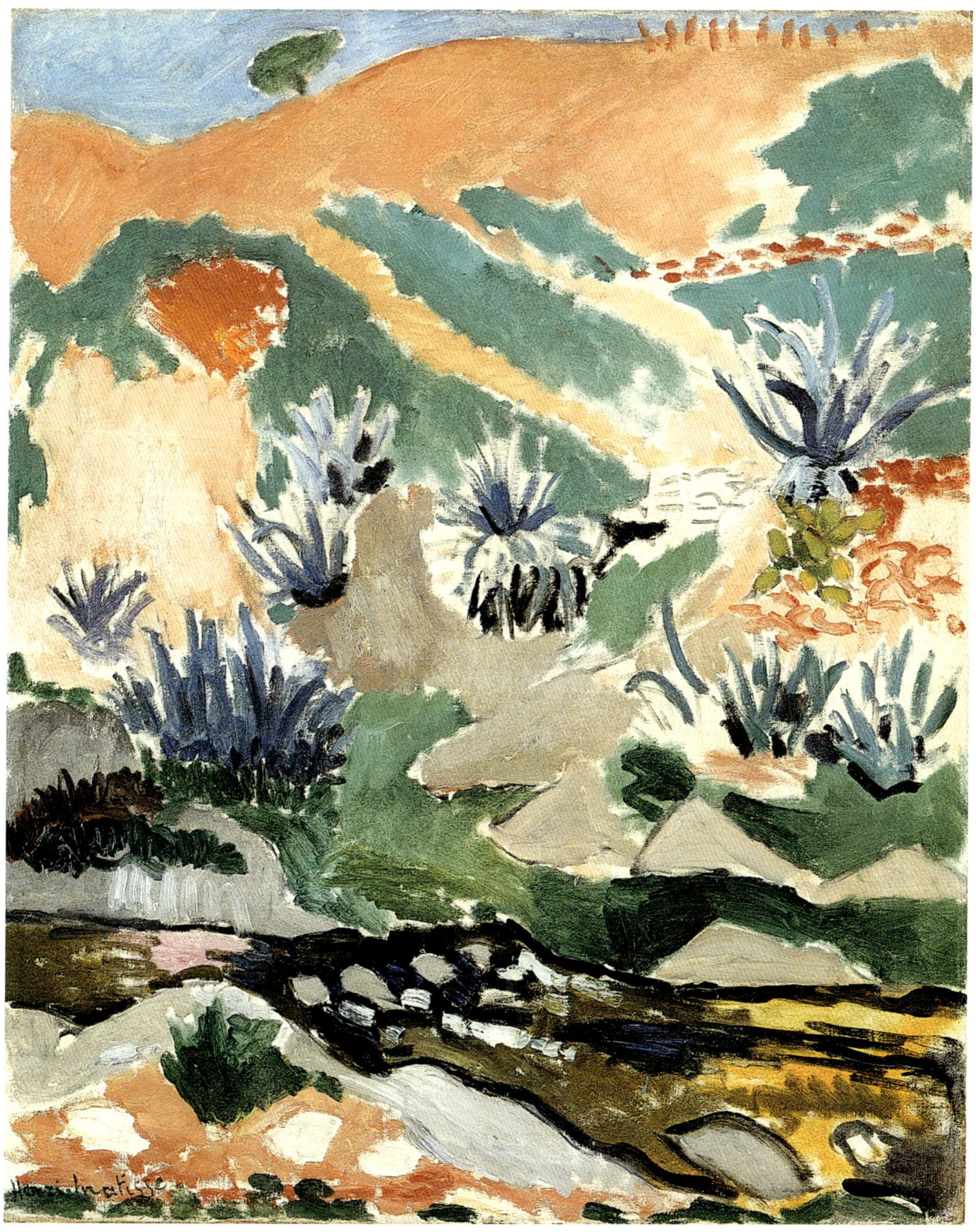

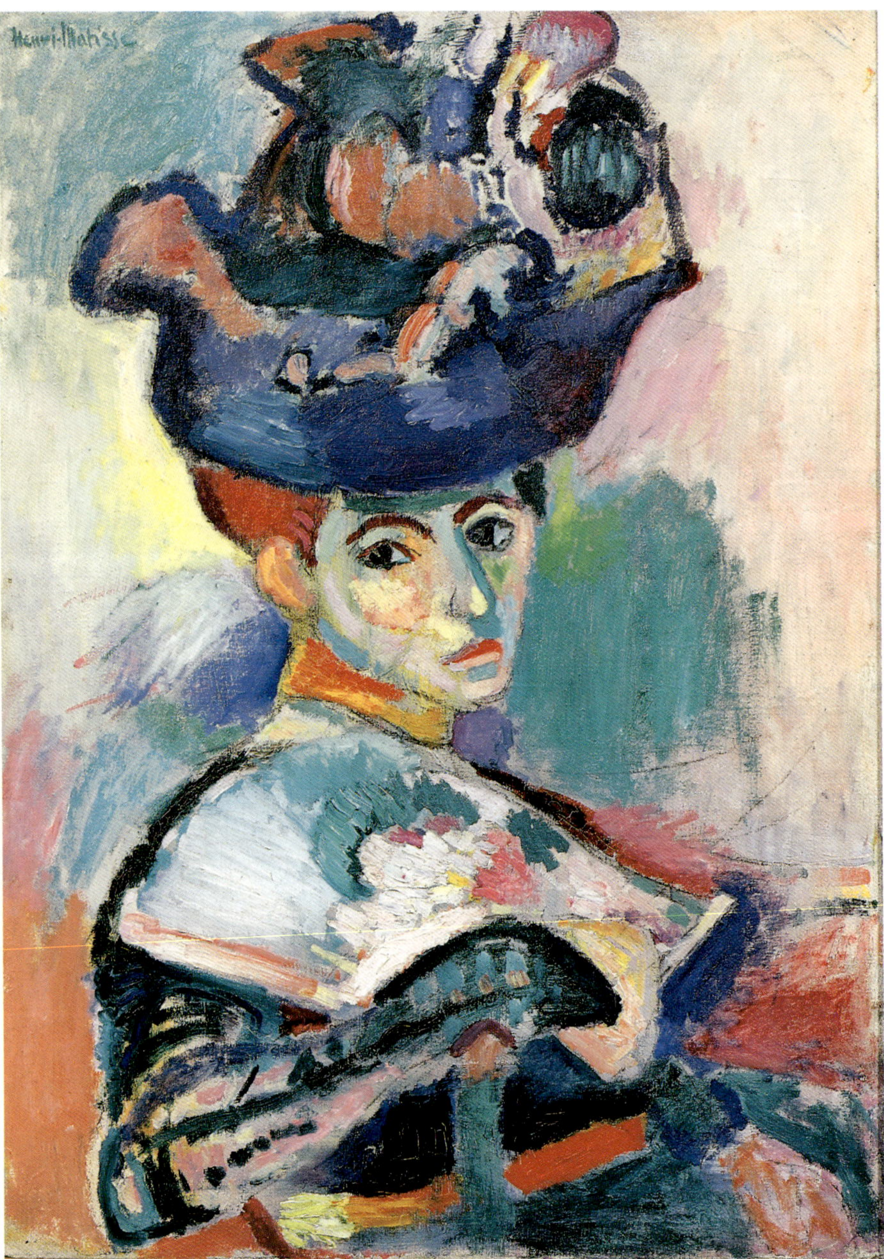
Henri-Matisse

I myself am fully convinced

that the best explanation an artist

can give of his aims and ability

is afforded by his work.

To copy the objects in a still life is nothing;
one must render the emotion they awaken in him.
The emotion of the ensemble, the interrelation of the objects,
the specific character of every object—modified by its relation
to the others—all interlaced like a cord or a serpent.

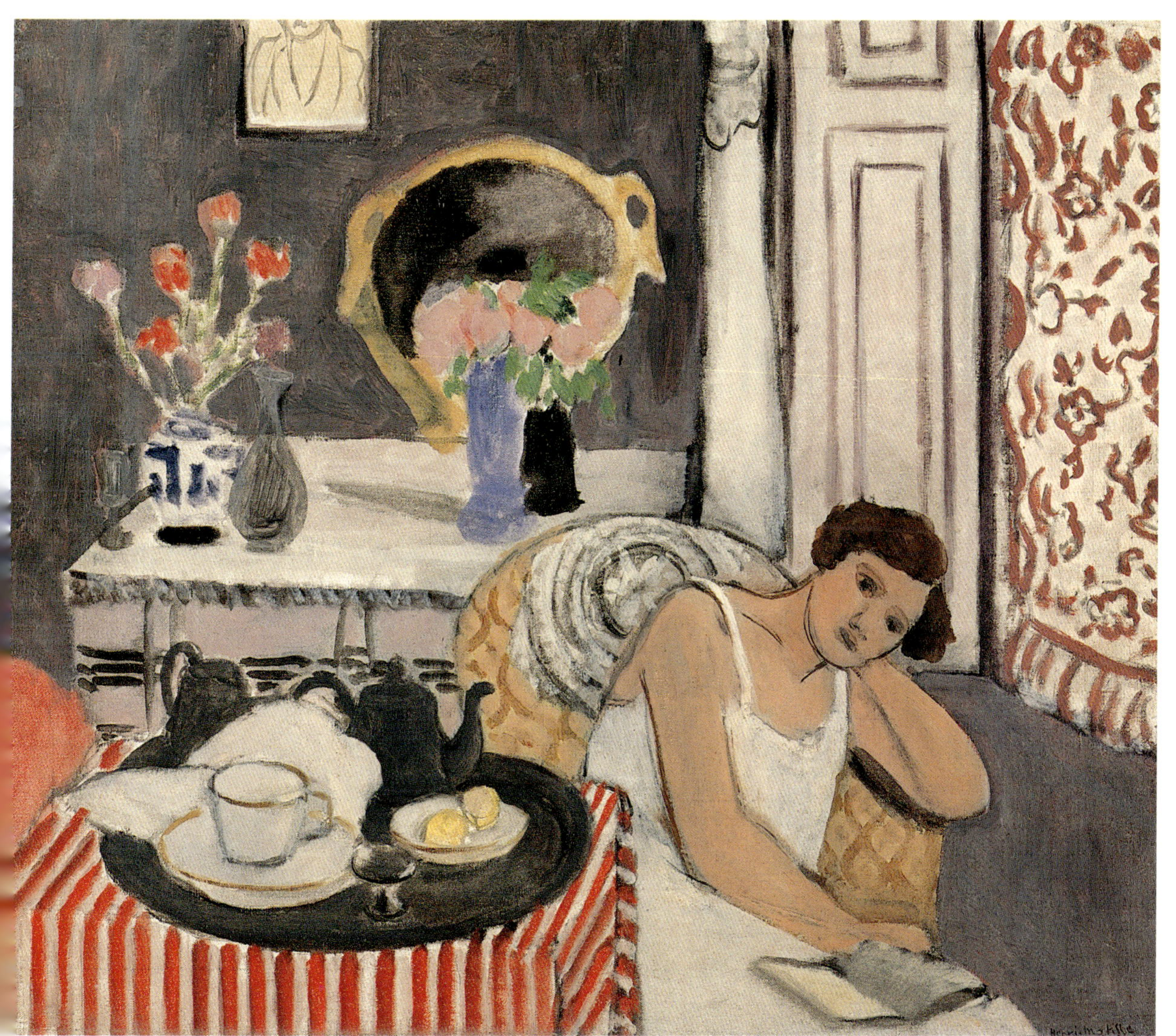

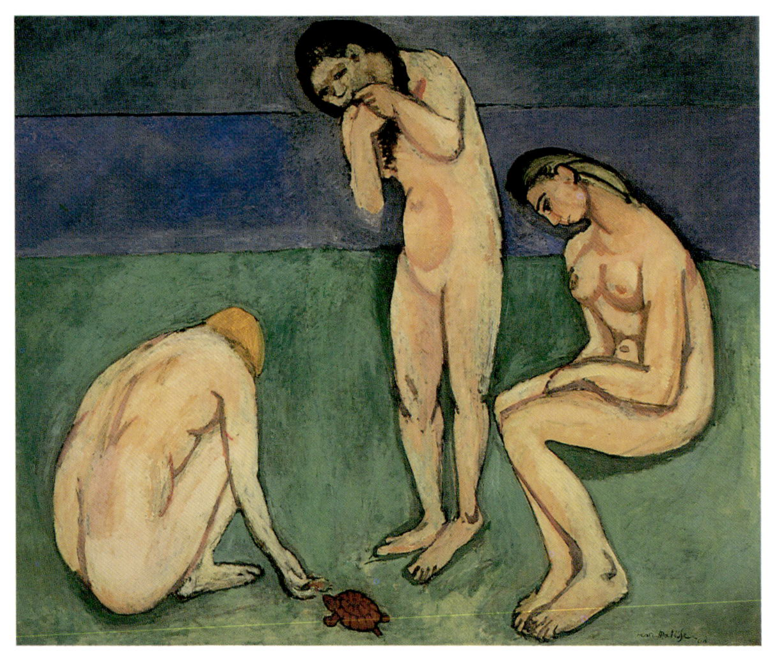

Fit your parts into one another and build up your figure as a carpenter does a house.

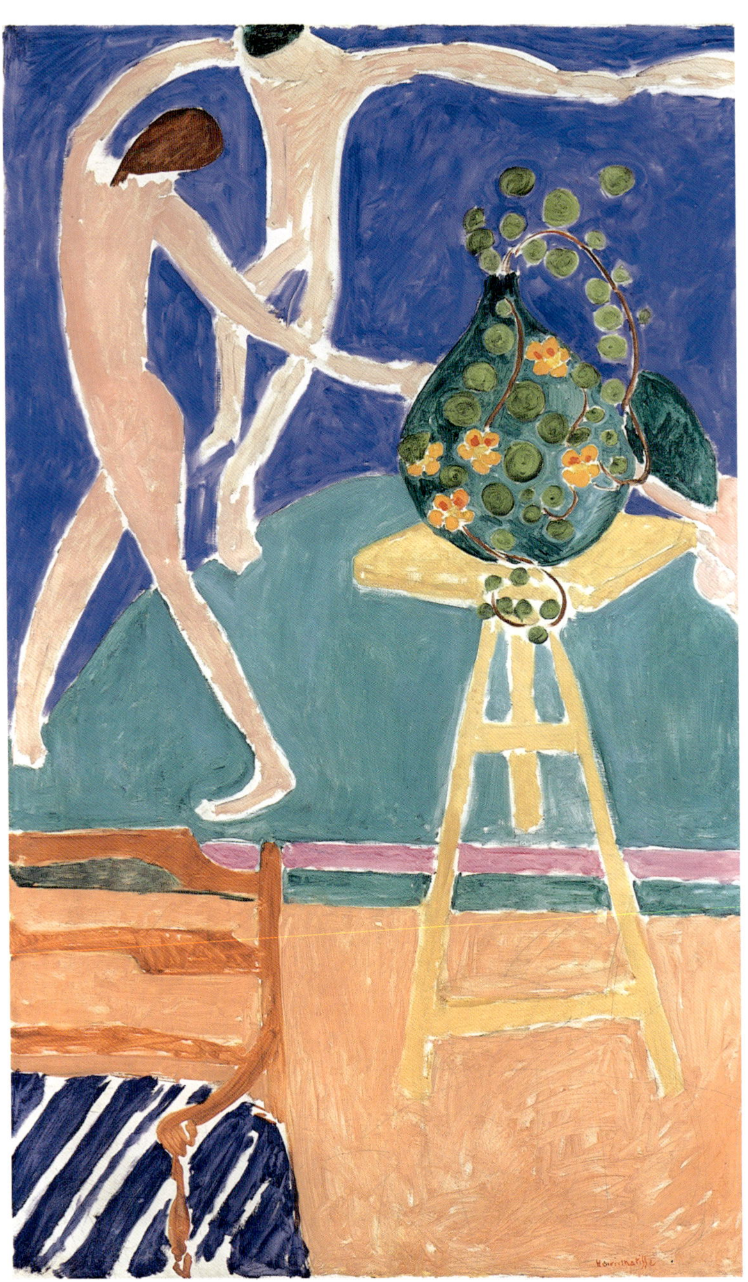

Happy are those who sing with all their heart, from the bottoms of their hearts. To find joy in the sky, the trees, the flowers. There are always flowers for those who want to see them.

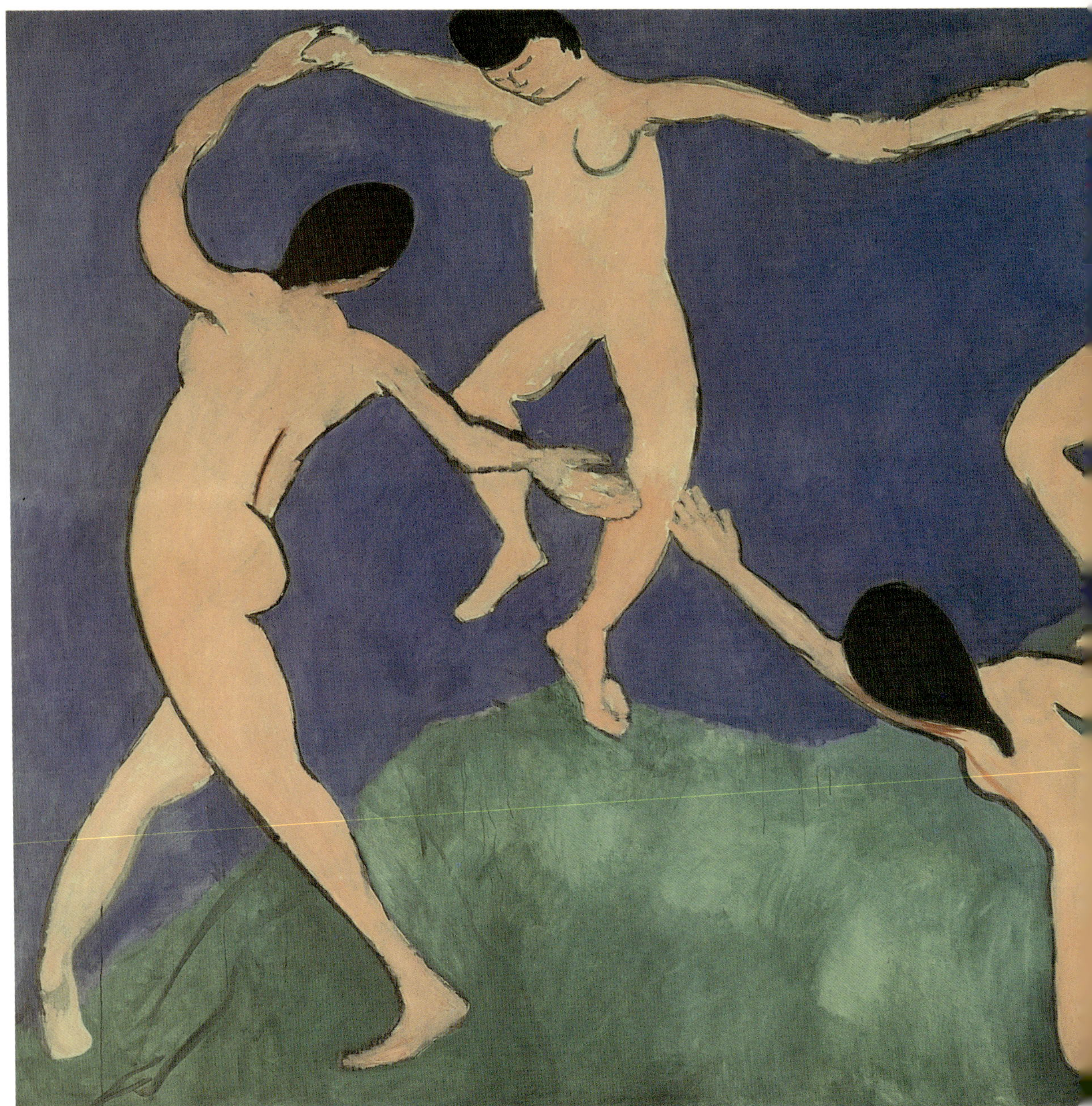

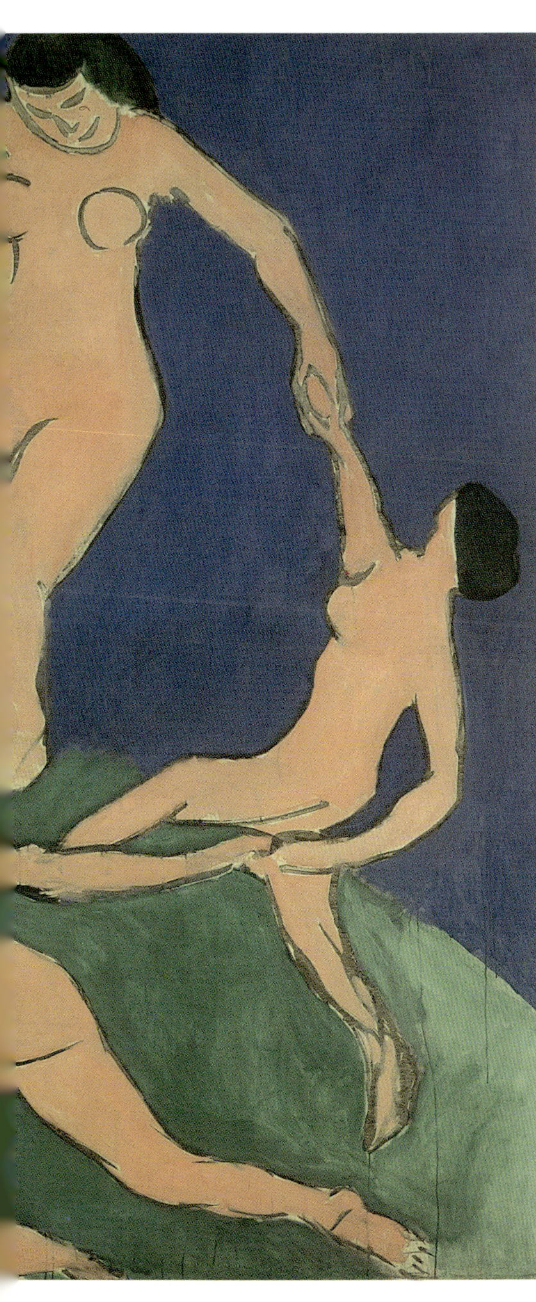

three colors . . .
blue for the sky,
pink for the bodies,
green for the hill.

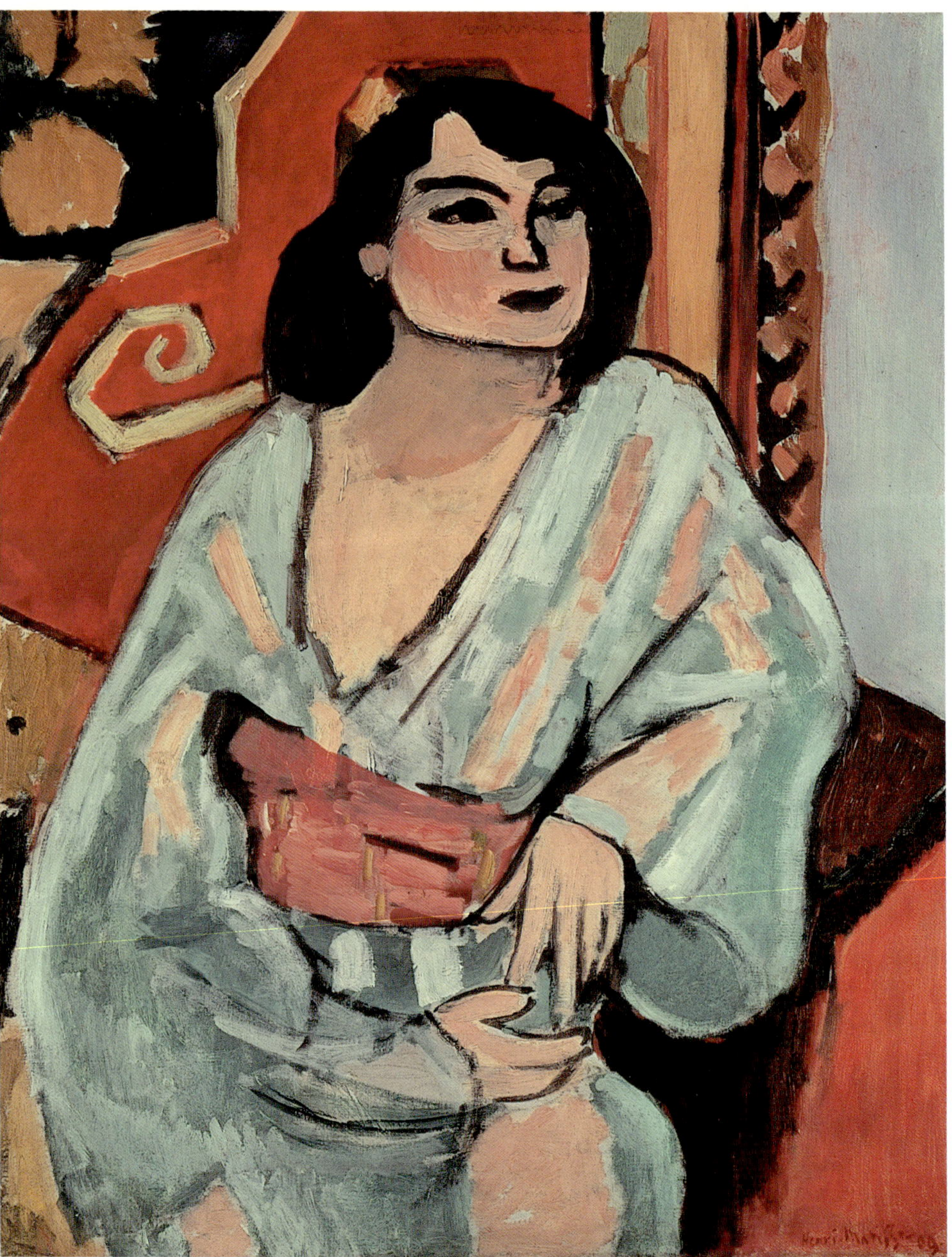

What is a portrait?

Is it not an interpretation

of the human sensibility

of the person represented?

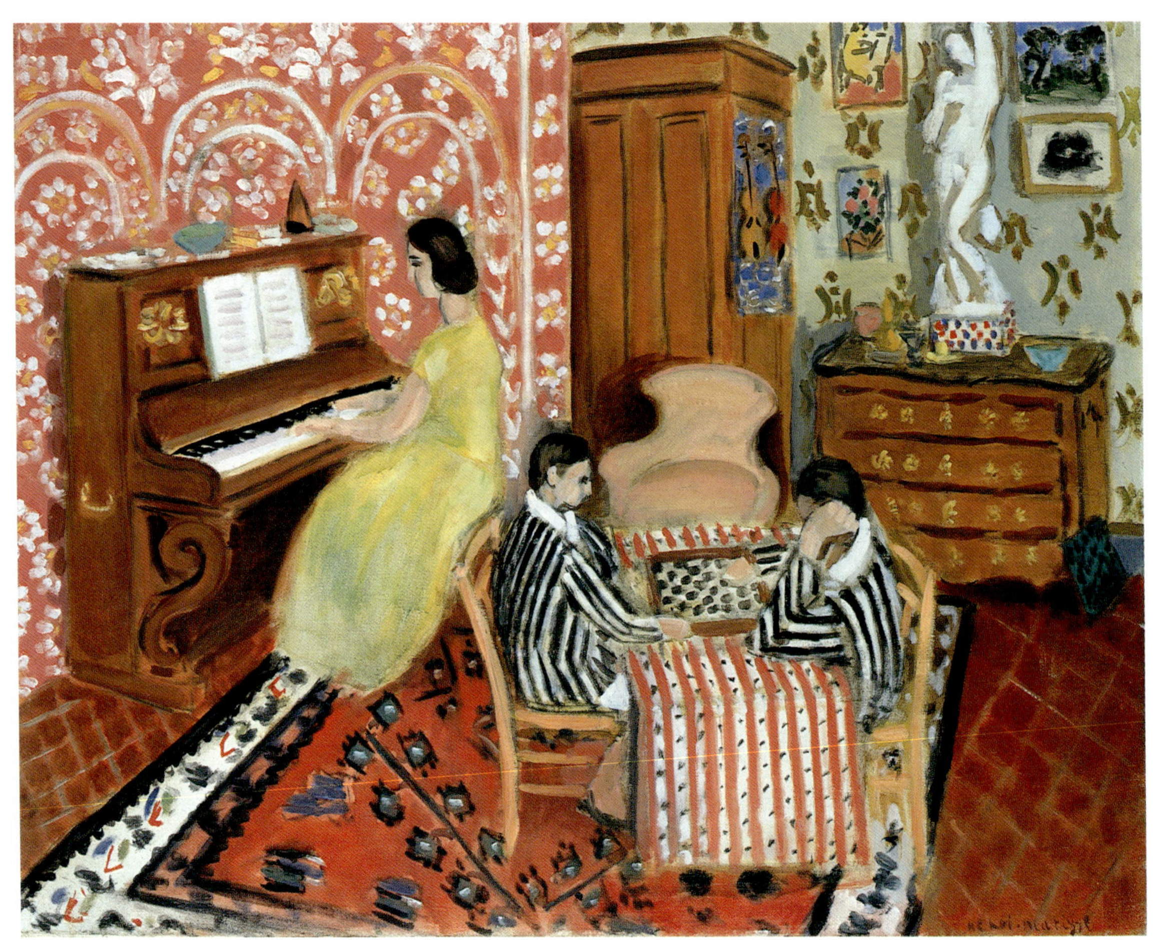

Composition is the art of arranging in a decorative manner the various elements at the painter's disposal for the expression of his feelings.

Slowly I discovered the secret of my art.
It consists of a meditation on nature, on the expression
of a dream which is always inspired by reality.

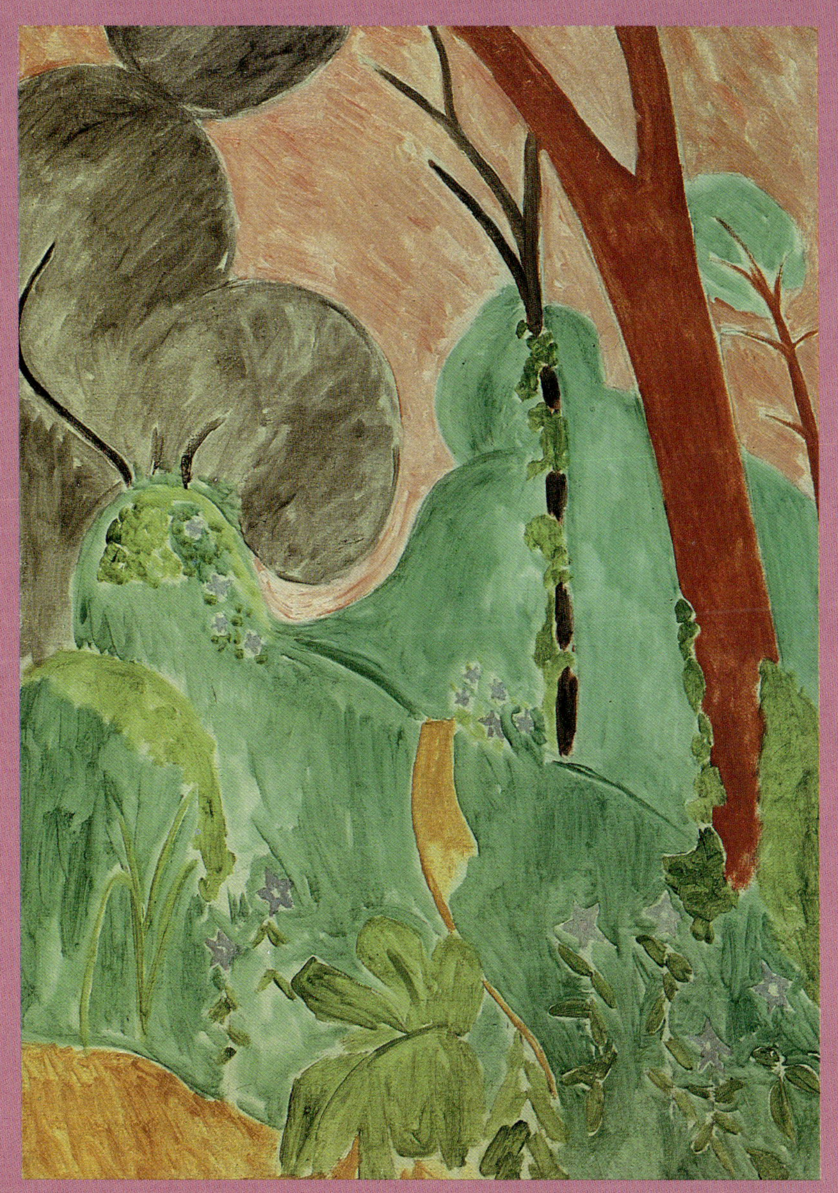

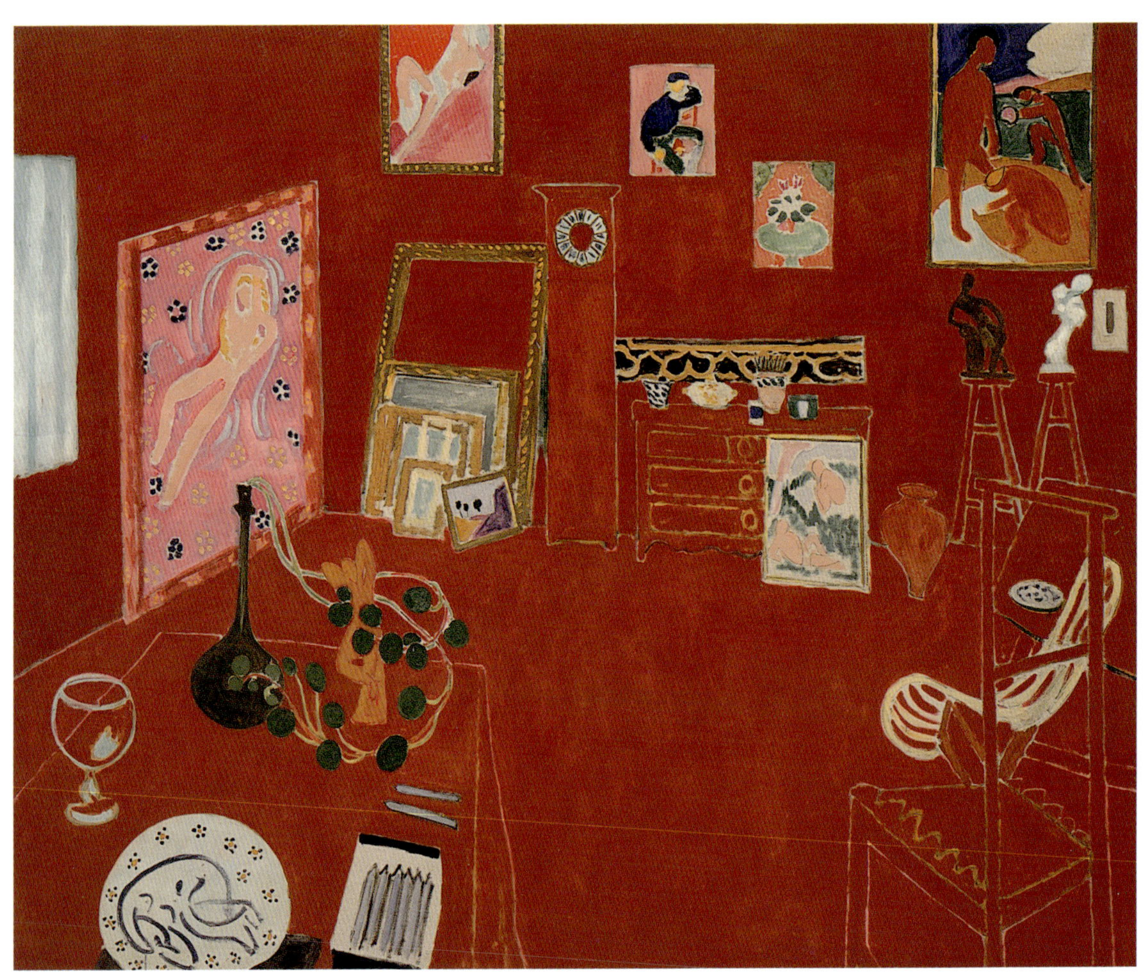

We have acquired a notion of limitless space, but we also find solace in the limited space of a room in our home full of the knickknacks that have accumulated in it through the years. Both points of view are not contradictory; they complement each other.

A new painting should be a unique thing,

a birth bringing a new face into

the representation of the world through

the human spirit. The artist should

call forth all of his energy, his sincerity,

and the greatest possible modesty

in order to push aside during his work

the old clichés that come so readily

to his hand and can suffocate

the small flower that itself

never turns out as one expected.

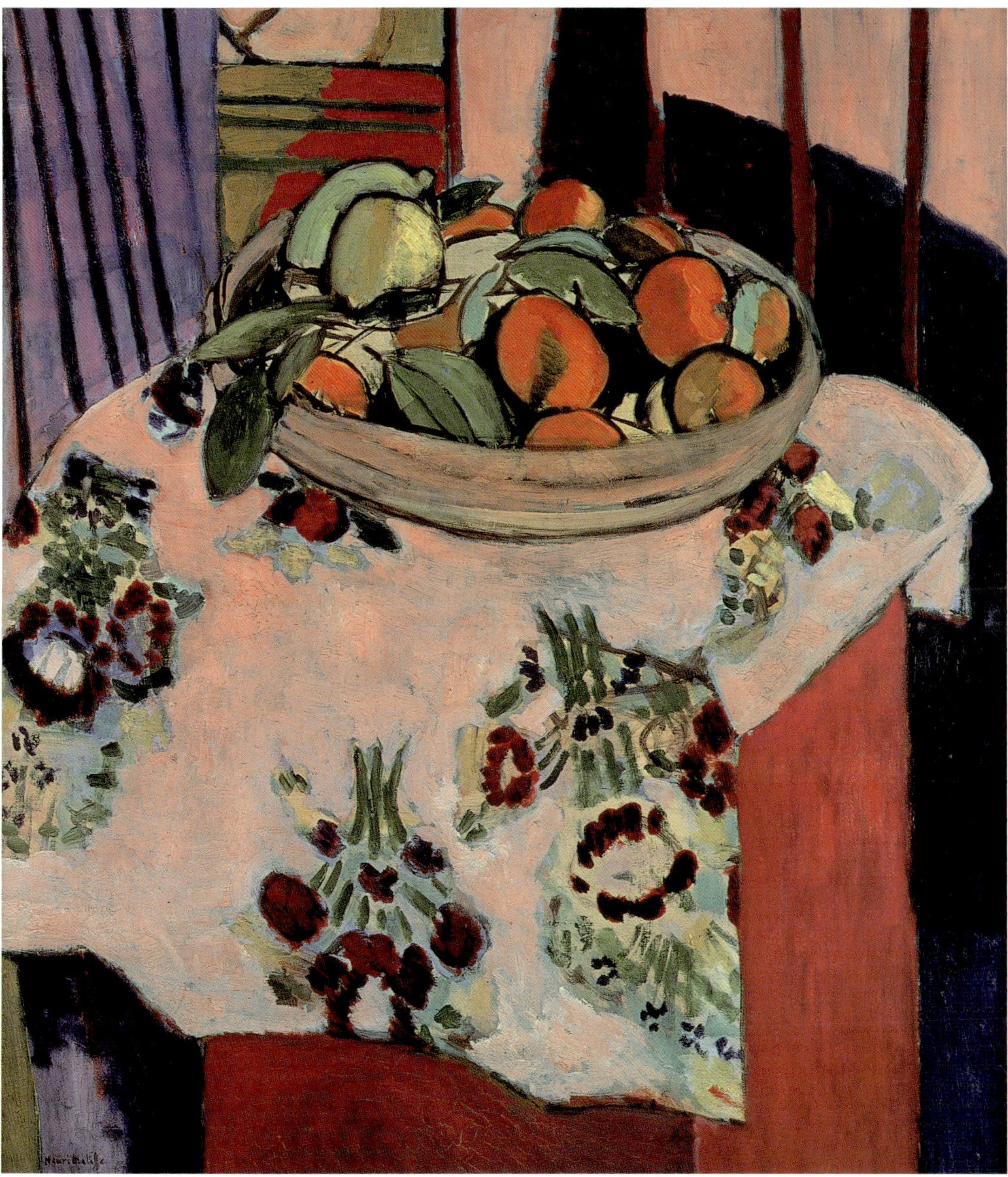

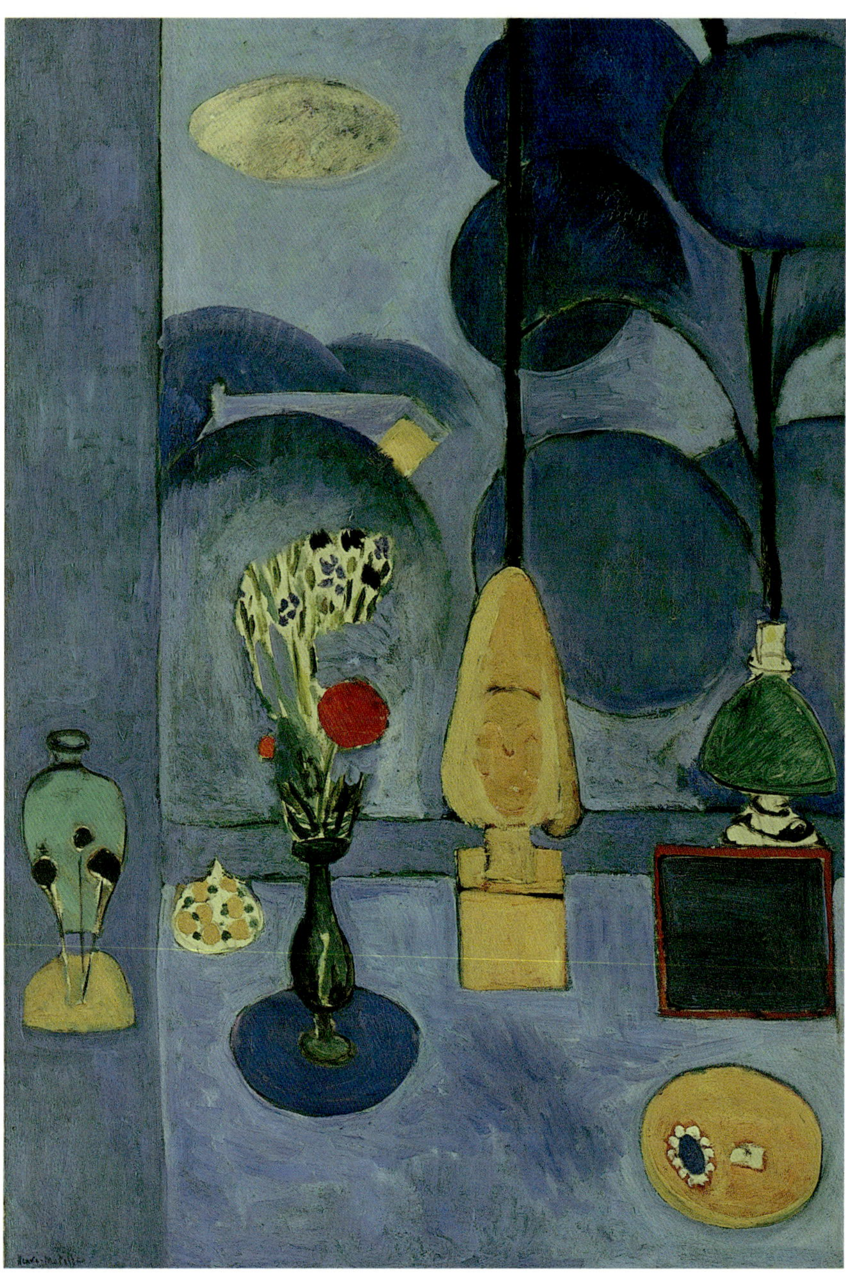

One can't live in a house too well kept.
One has to go off into the jungle to find simpler
ways which won't stifle the spirit.

When I make my drawings . . .

the path traced by my pencil

on the sheet of paper is,

to some extent, analogous

to the gesture of a man

groping his way in the darkness.

I mean that there is nothing

foreseen about my path:

I am led. I do not lead.

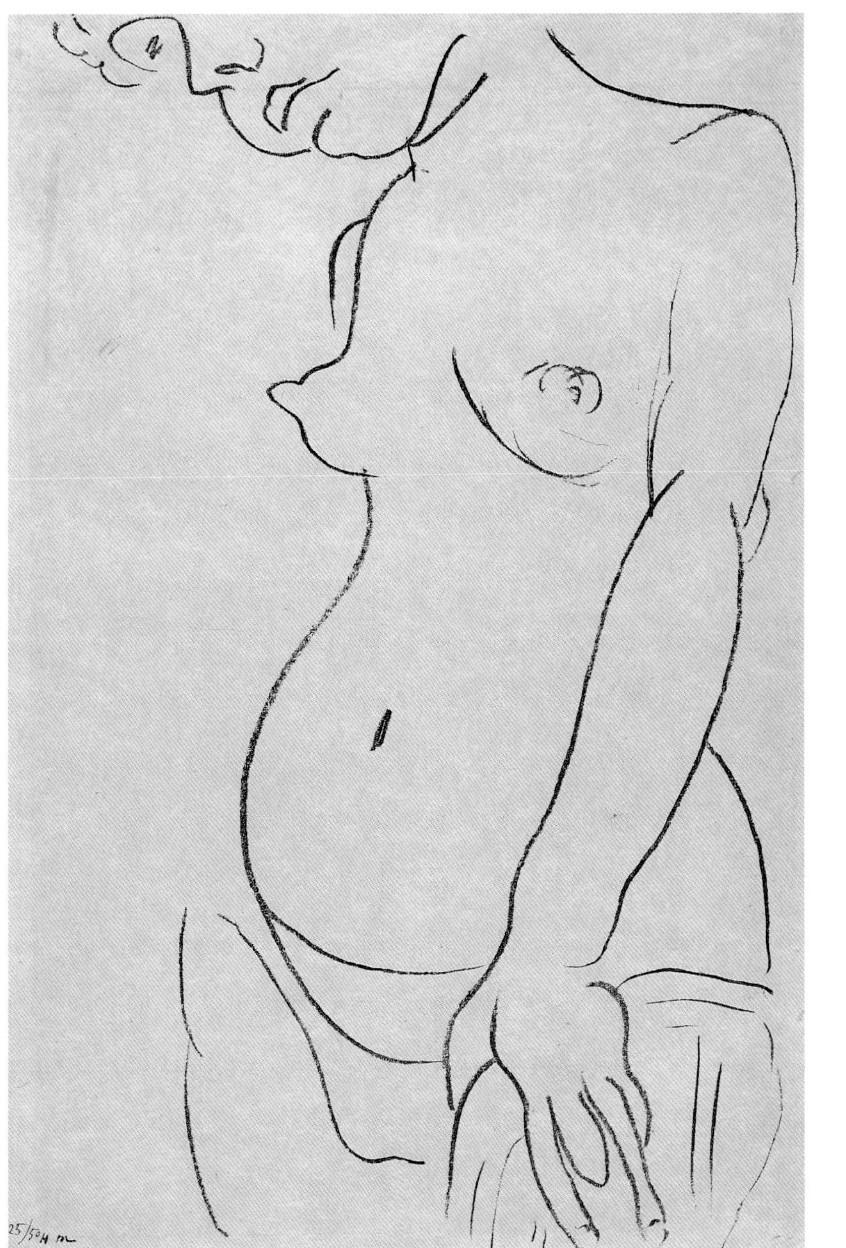

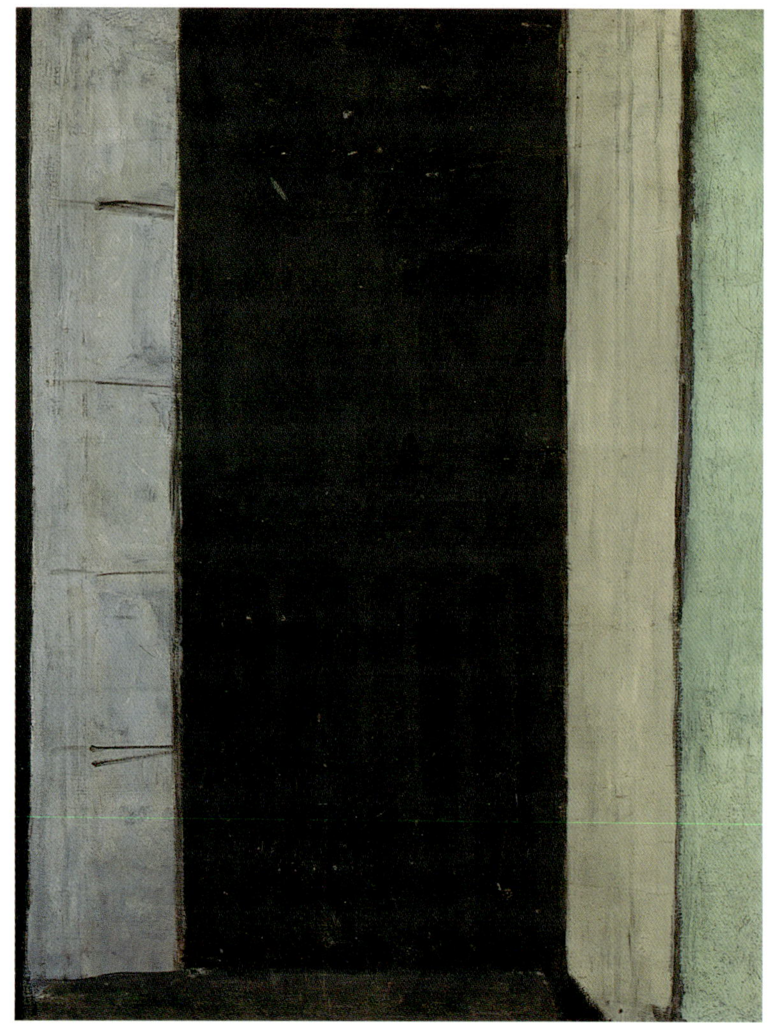

All that is not useful in

the picture is detrimental.

A work of art must be

harmonious in its entirety.

What I dream of is an art of balance, of purity and serenity.

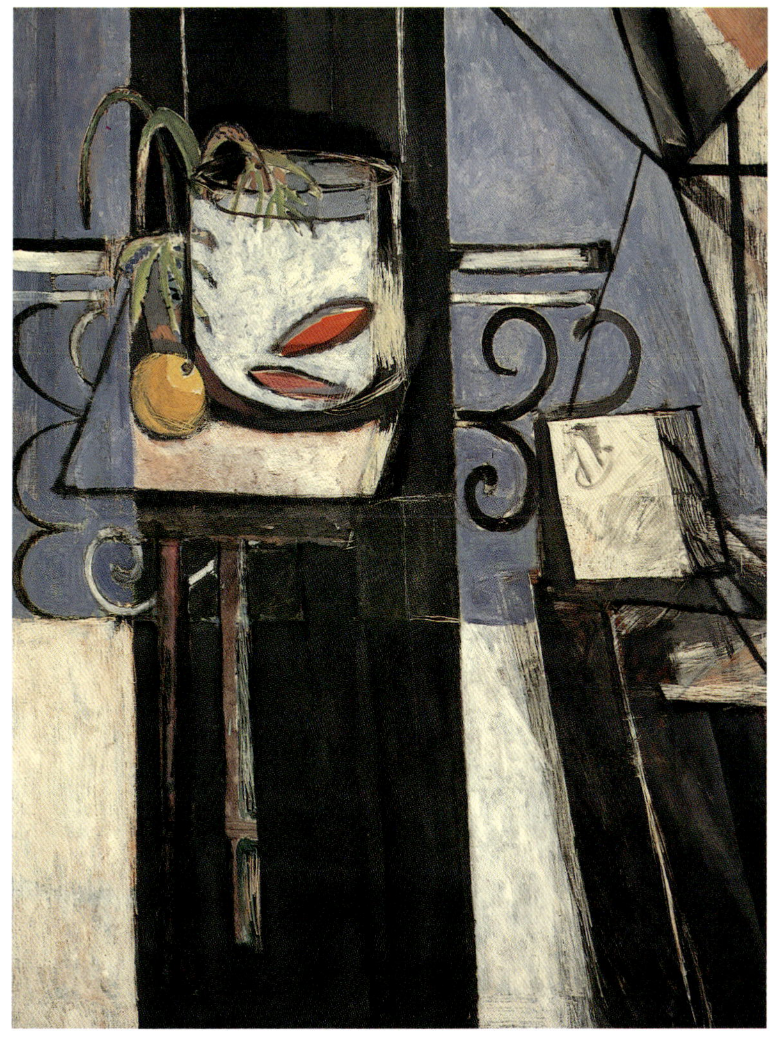

Sometimes I stop in front of a motif,
a corner of my studio which I find
expressive, yet quite beyond myself and
my strength and I await the thunderbolt
which cannot fail to come.

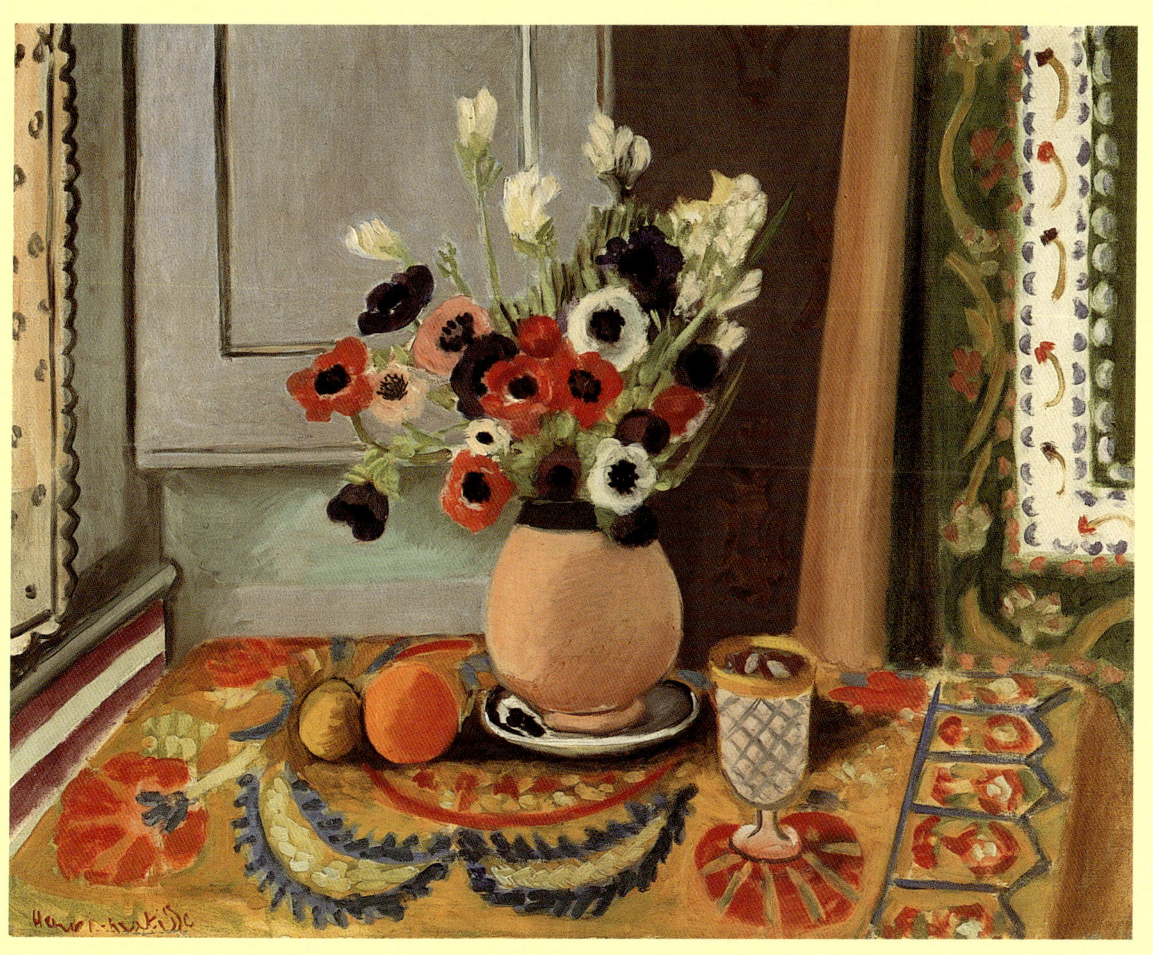

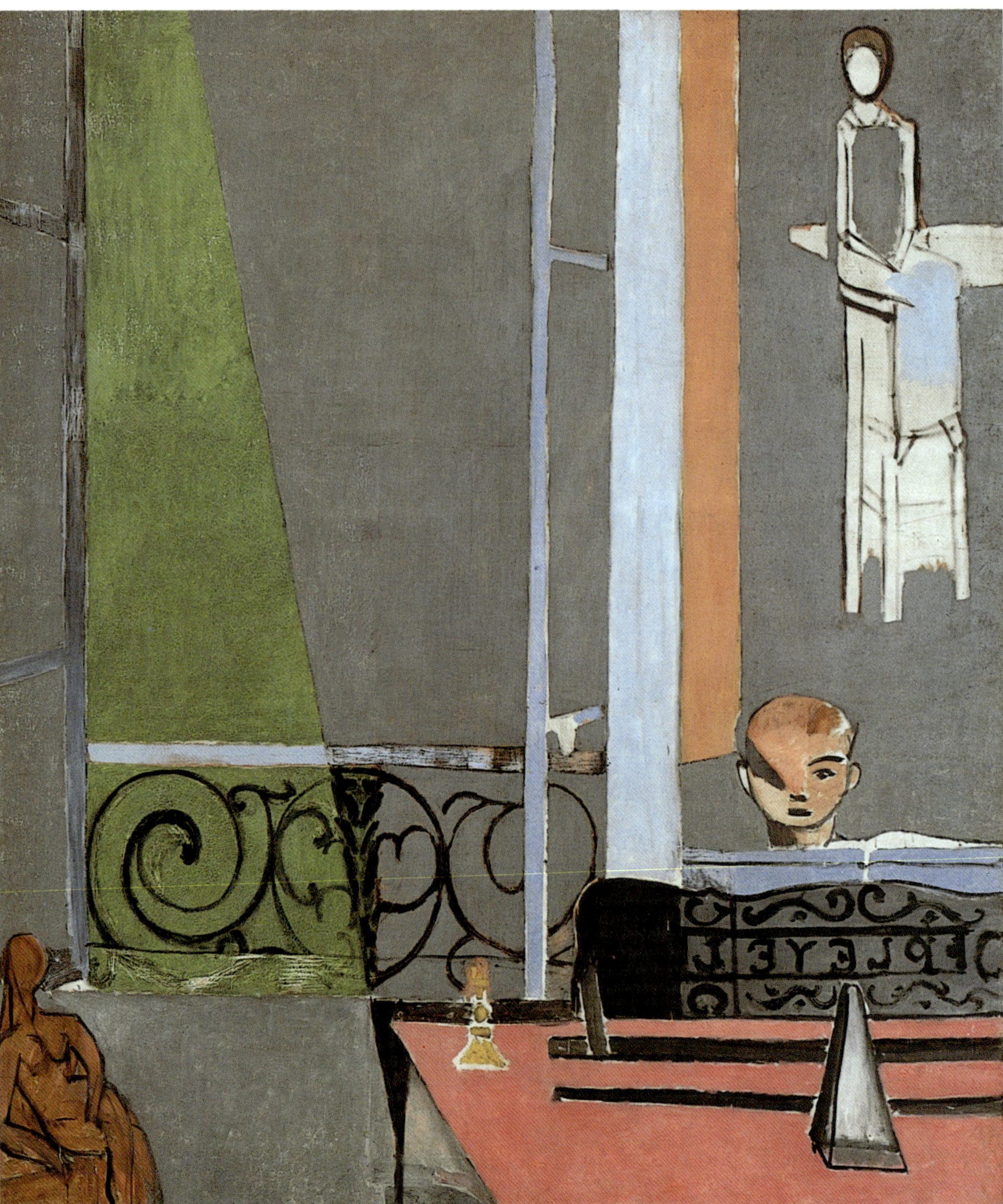

I always dreamed of other proportions that might be found in the other hemisphere.

I was always conscious of another space in which the objects of my reveries evolved.

I was seeking something other than real space.

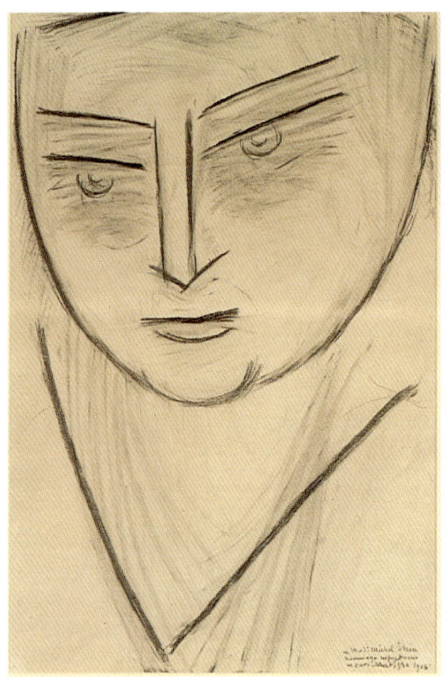

. . . a line cannot exist alone; it always brings a companion along.

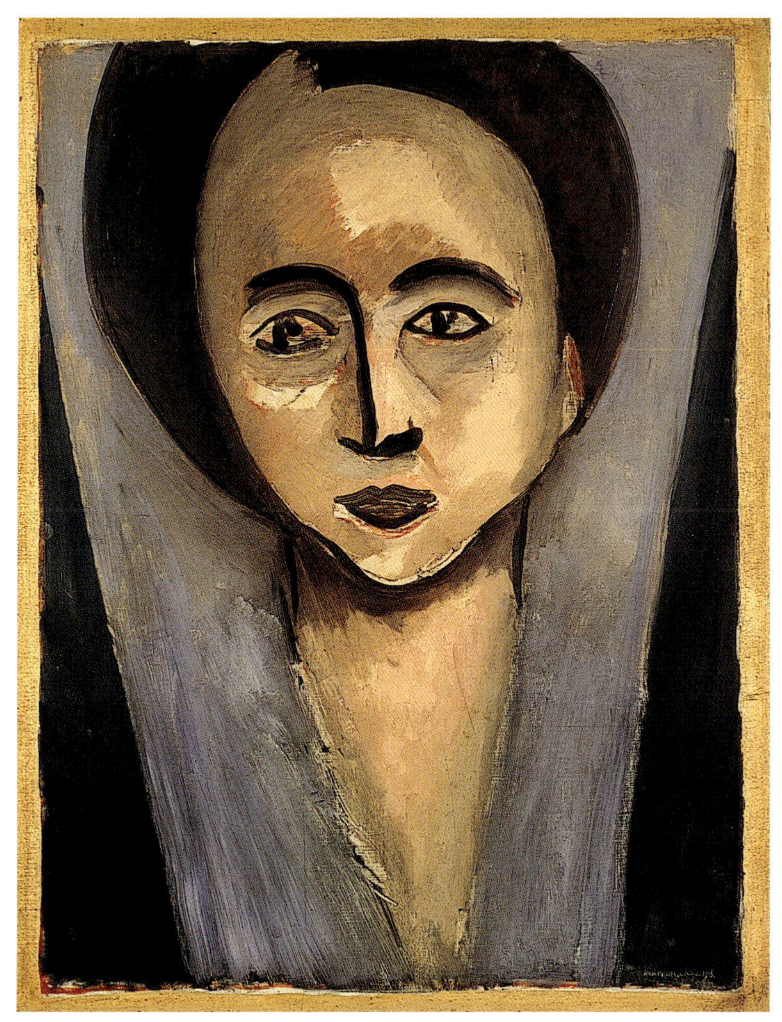

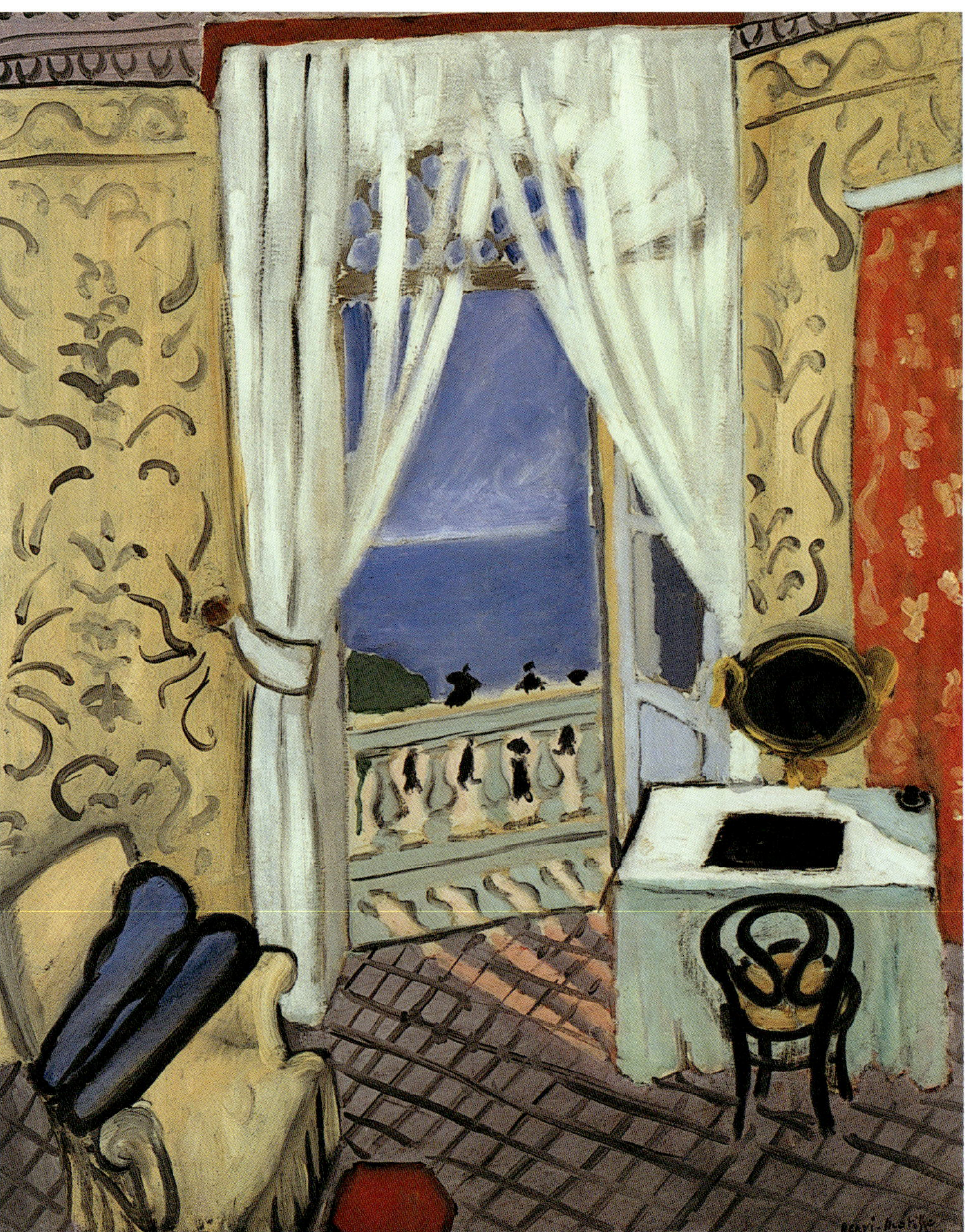

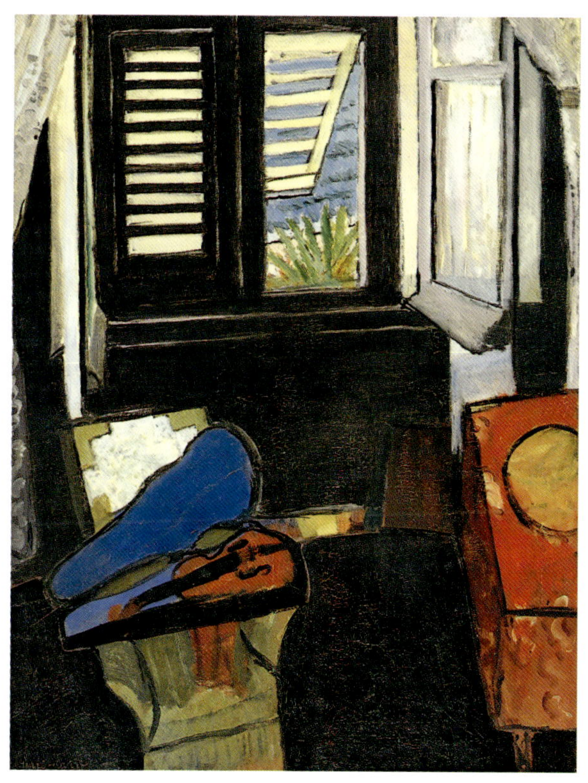

A painter doesn't see everything that he has put in his paintings. It is other people who find these treasures in it, one by one, and the richer a painting is in surprises of this sort, in treasures, the greater its author.

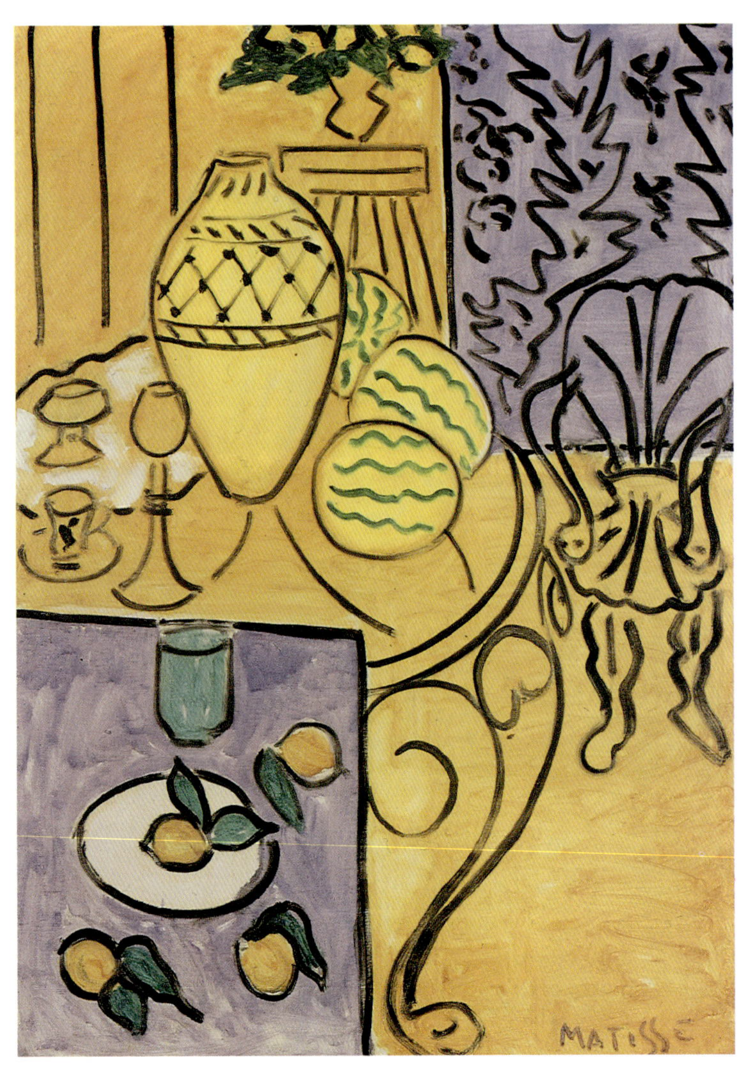
MATISSE

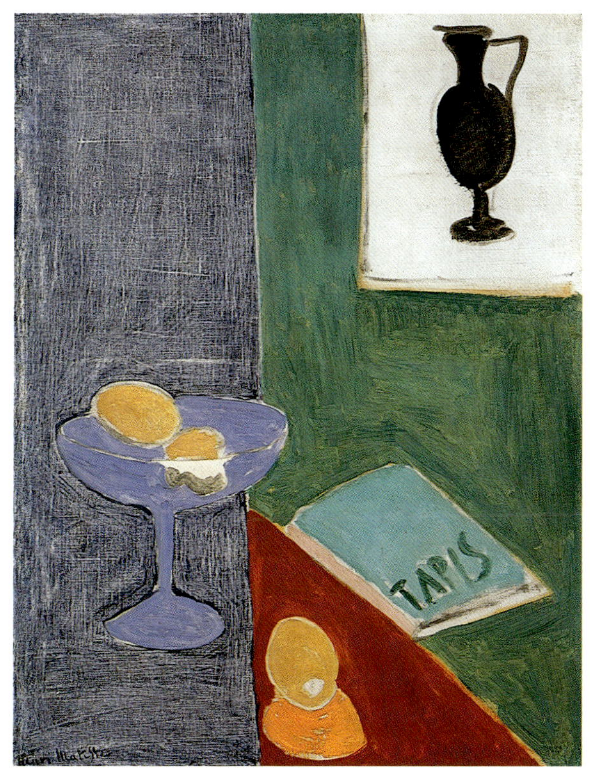

Those who work in an affected style, deliberately turning their backs on nature, are in error—an artist must recognize that when he uses his reason, his picture is an artifice and that when he paints, he must feel that he is copying nature—and even when he consciously departs from nature, he must do it with the conviction that it is only the better to interpret her.

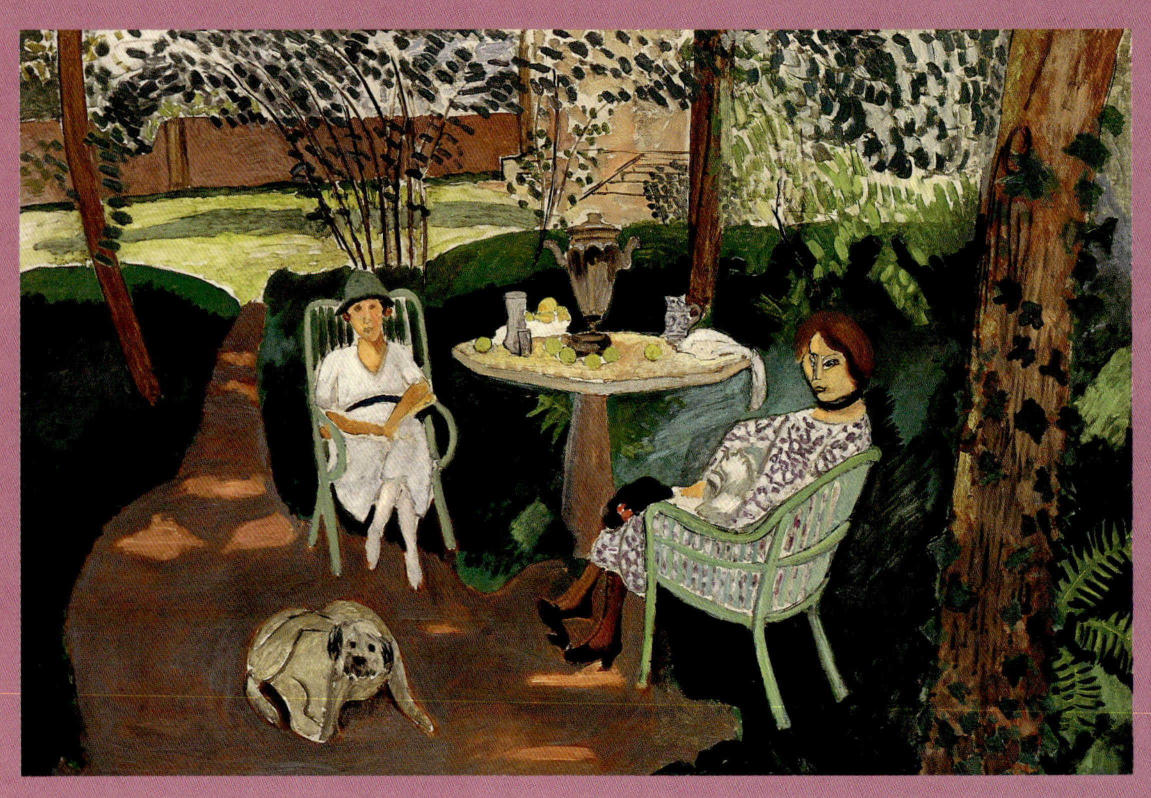

Charm, lightness, crispness—all these are passing sensations.
I have a canvas on which the colors are still fresh and I begin work on it again.
The colors will probably grow heavier—the freshness of the original tones
will give way to greater solidity, an improvement to my mind,
but less seductive to the eye.

My reaction at each stage is as important as the subject.

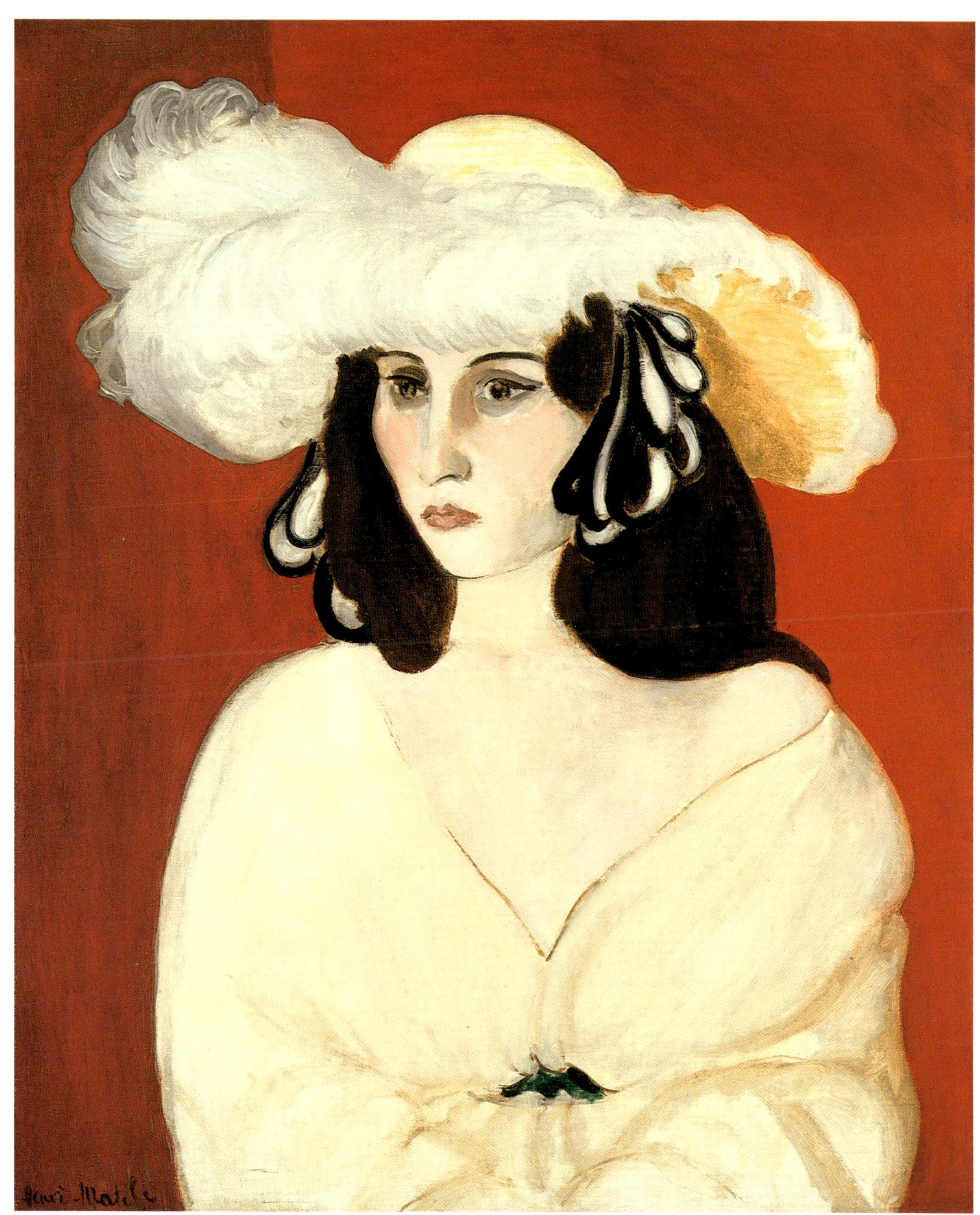

What interests me most

is neither still life nor landscape

but the human figure.

It is through it

that I best succeed in expressing

the nearly religious feeling

that I have towards life.

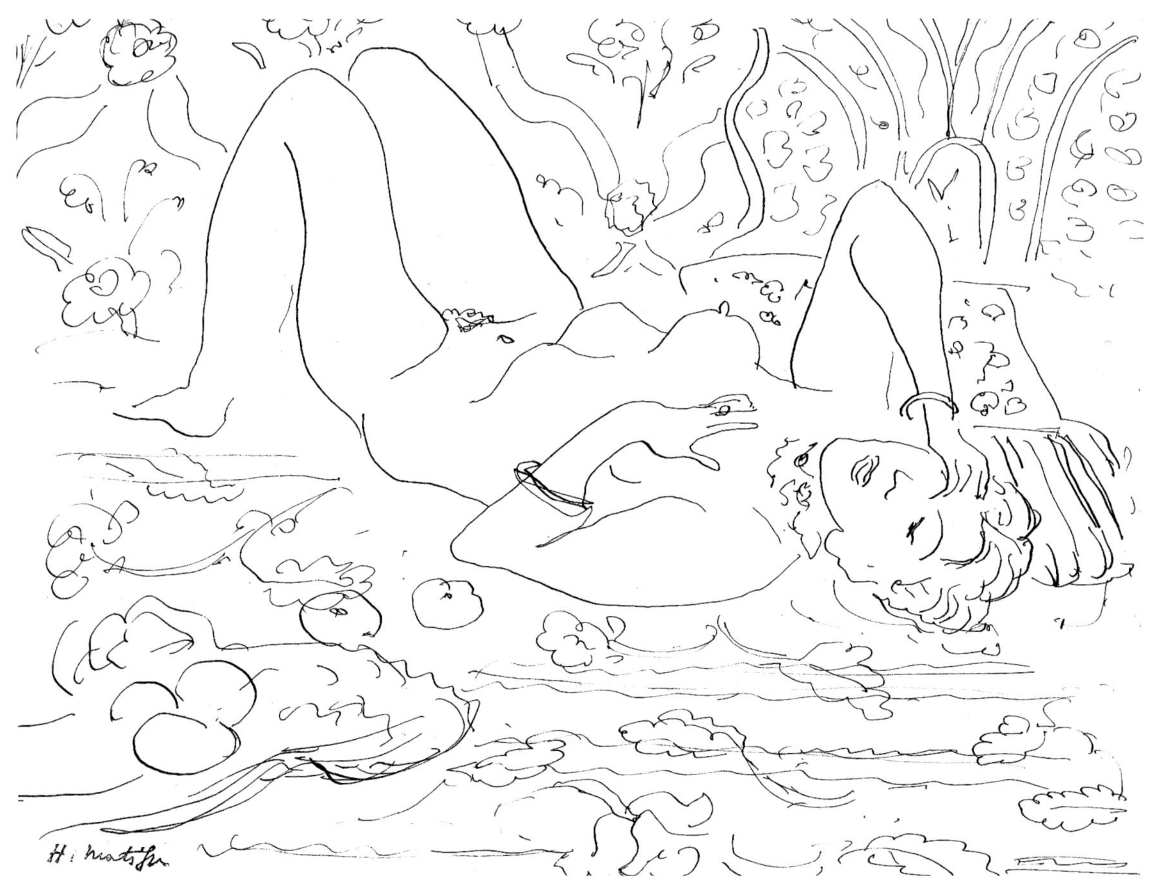
H. Matisse

Above all, I do not create a woman, I make a picture.

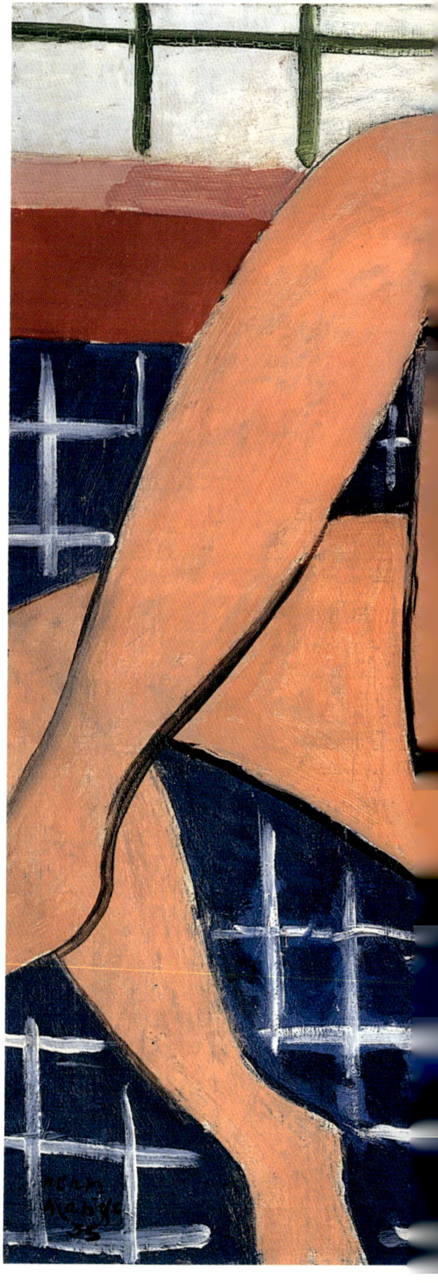

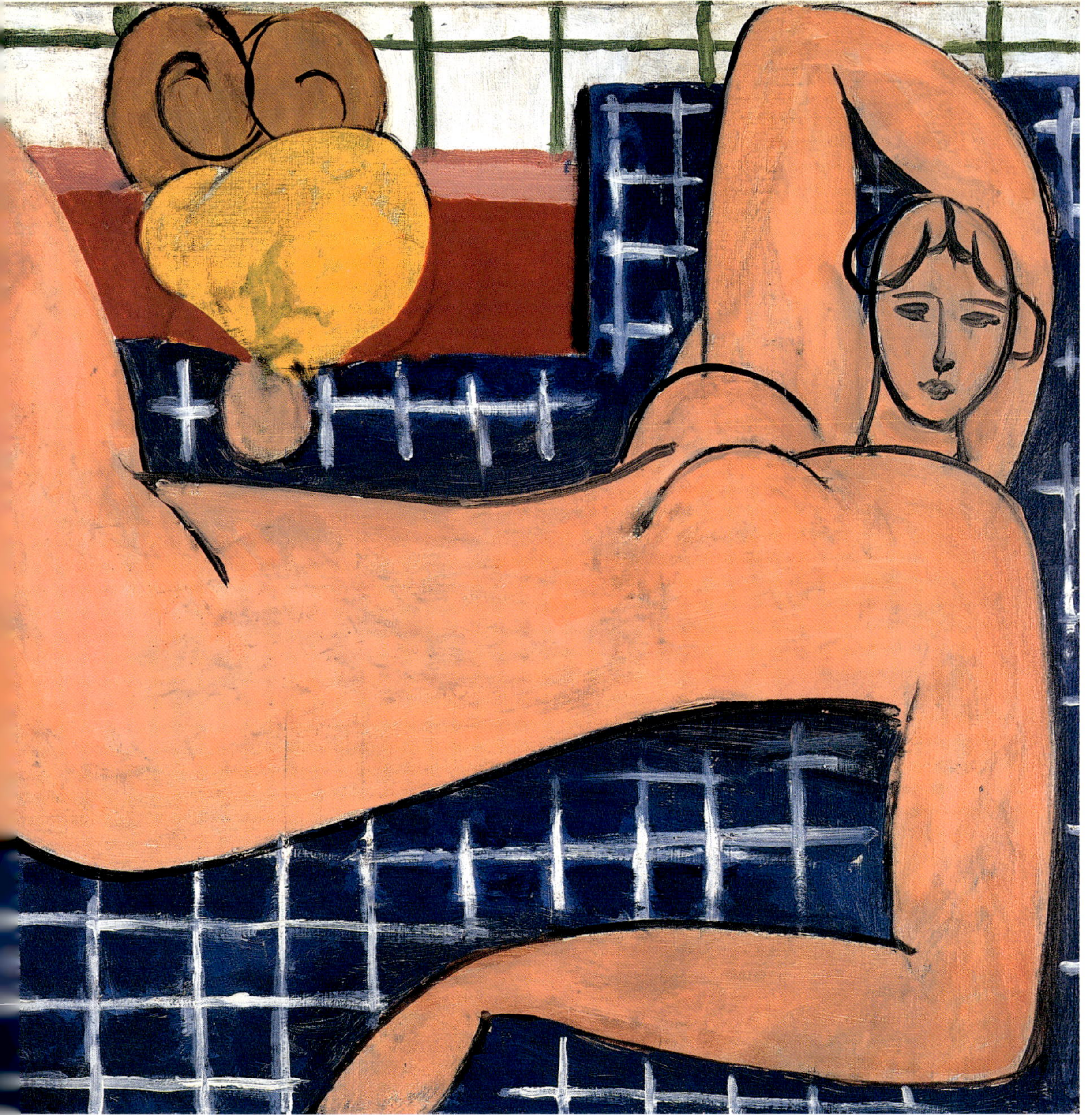

Painters, and I in particular, are not clever
at translating their feelings into words . . .

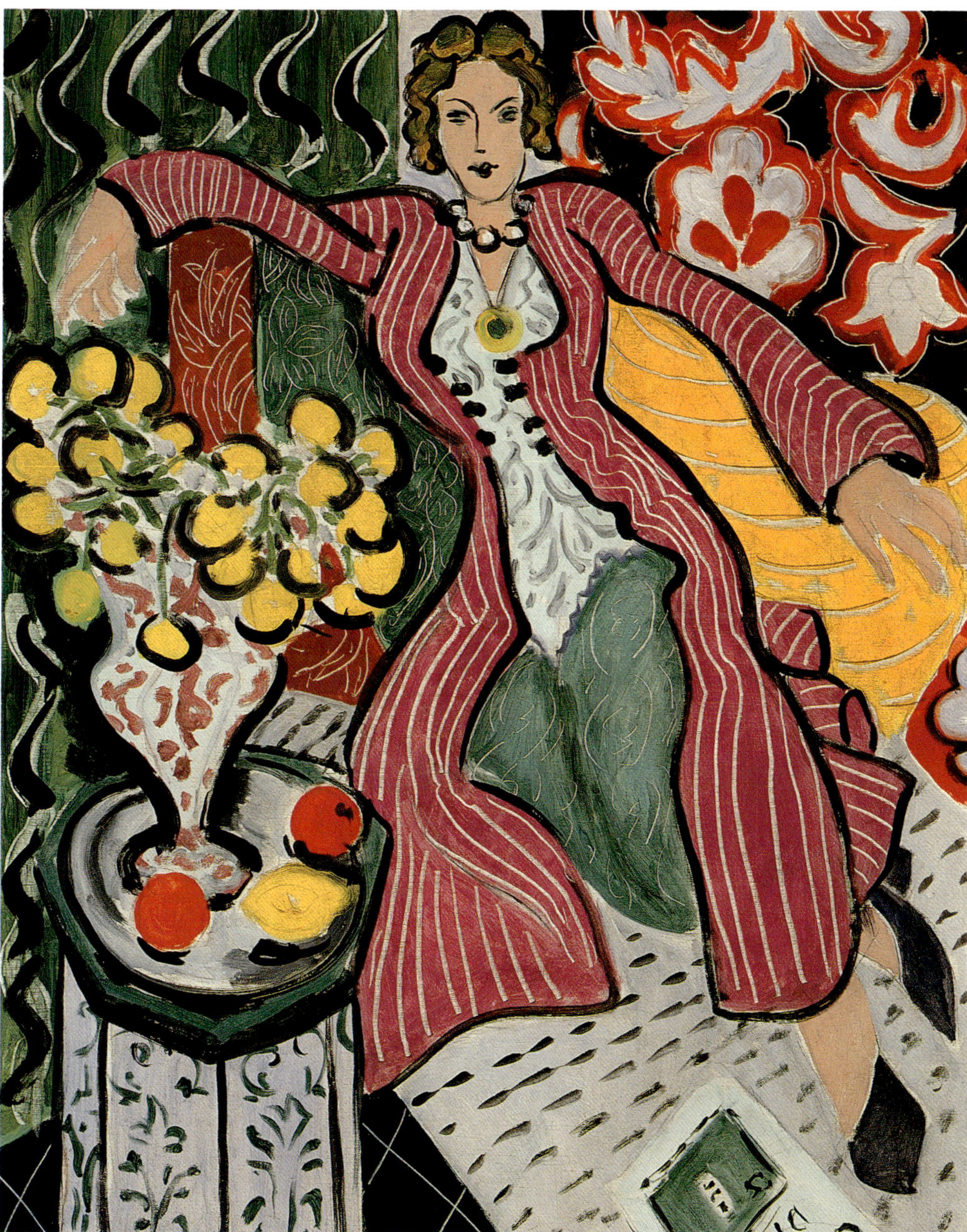

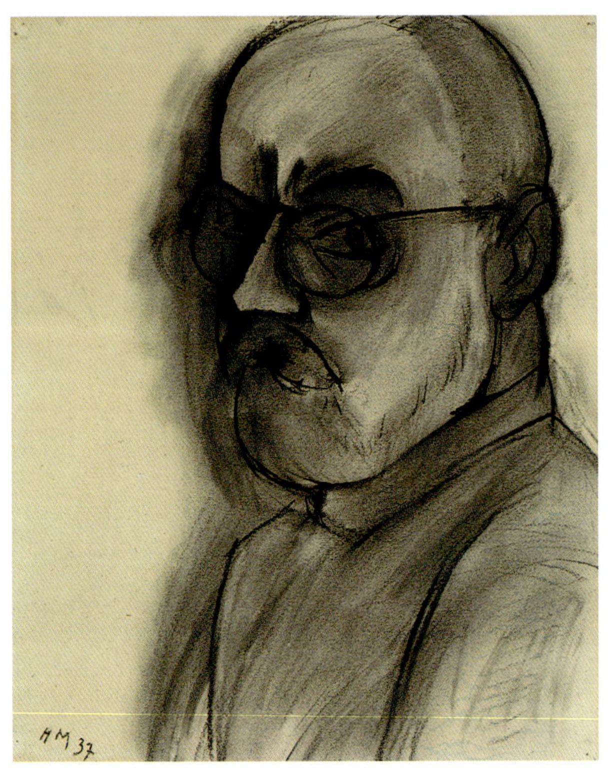
HM 37

It is quite clear that this sum total of elements describes the same man, as to his character and his personality, his way of looking at things and his reaction to life, and as to the reserve with which he faces it and which keeps him from an uncontrolled surrender to it. It is indeed the same man, one who always remains an attentive spectator of life and of himself.

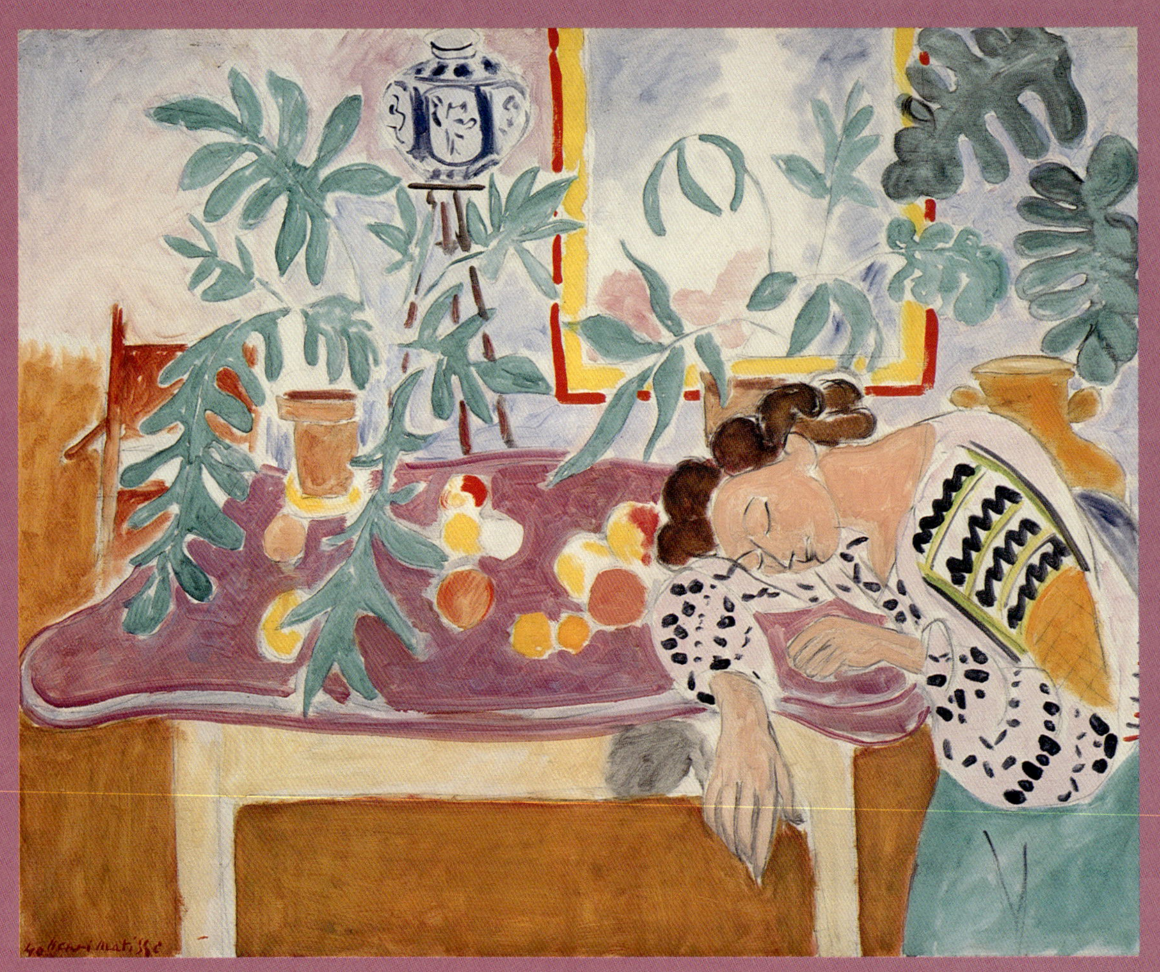

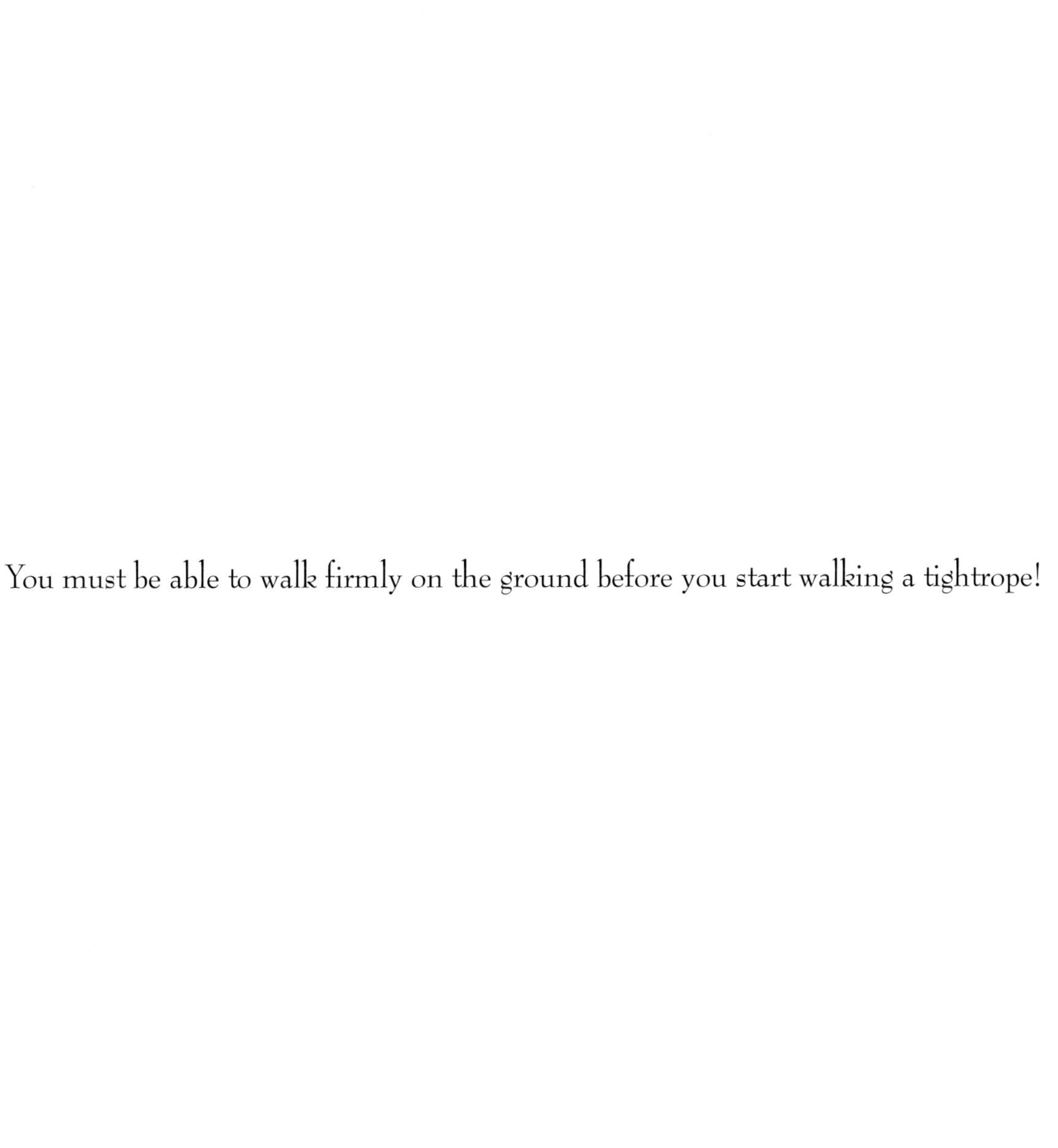

You must be able to walk firmly on the ground before you start walking a tightrope!

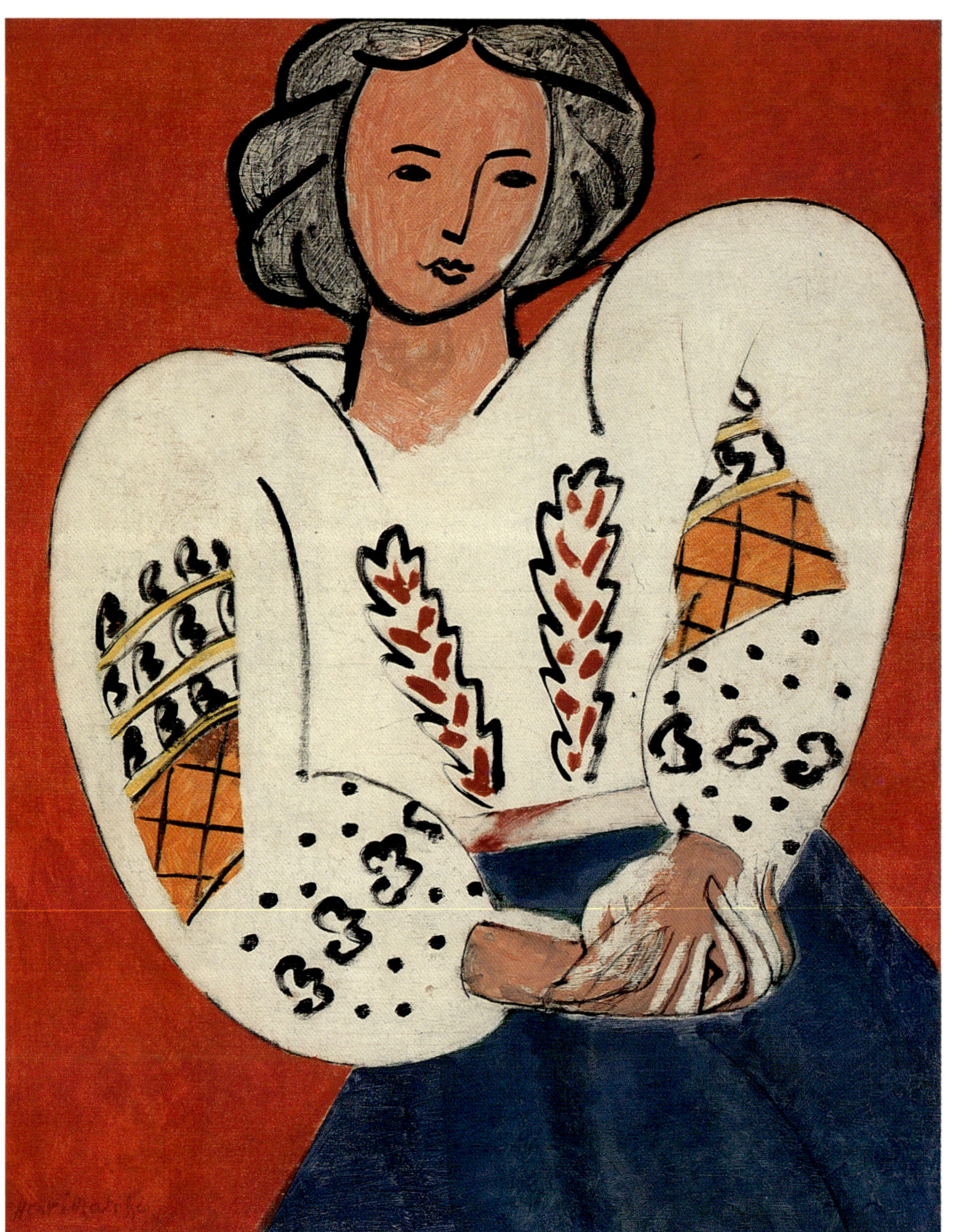

I do not insist upon the details of the face.

A work of art must carry in itself its
complete significance and impose it upon the beholder
even before he can identify the subject matter.

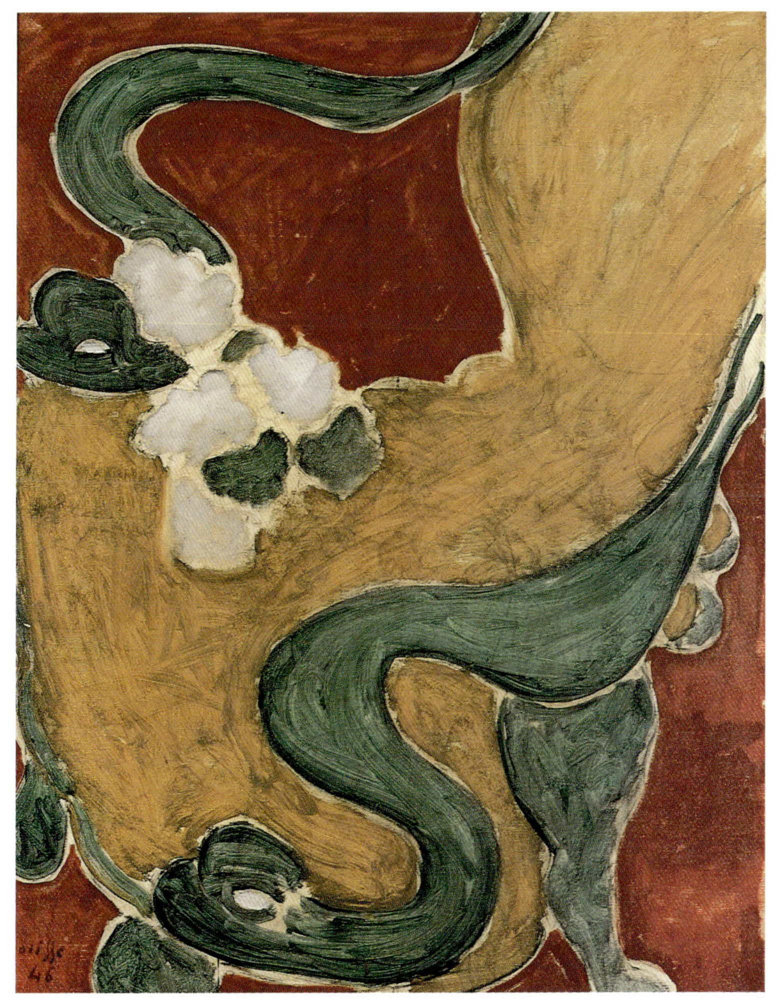

What I am after, above all, is expression.

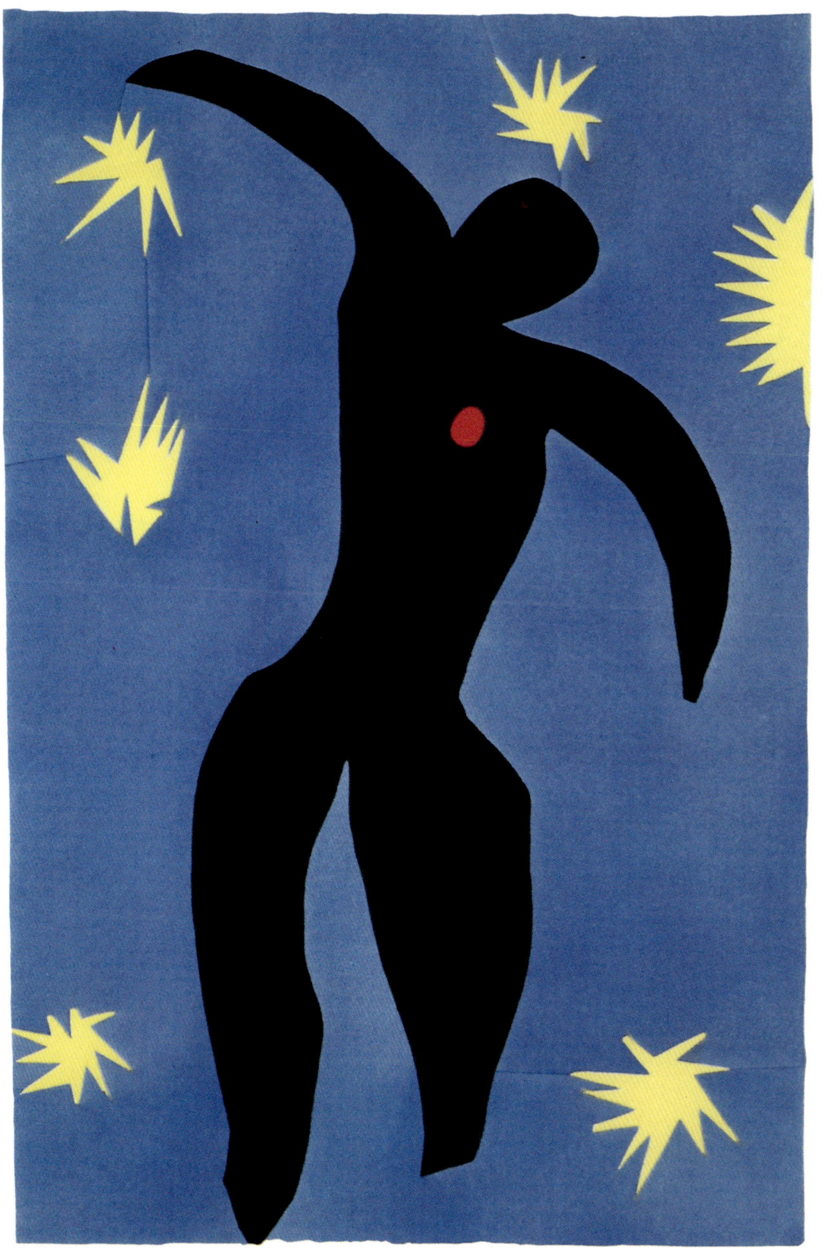

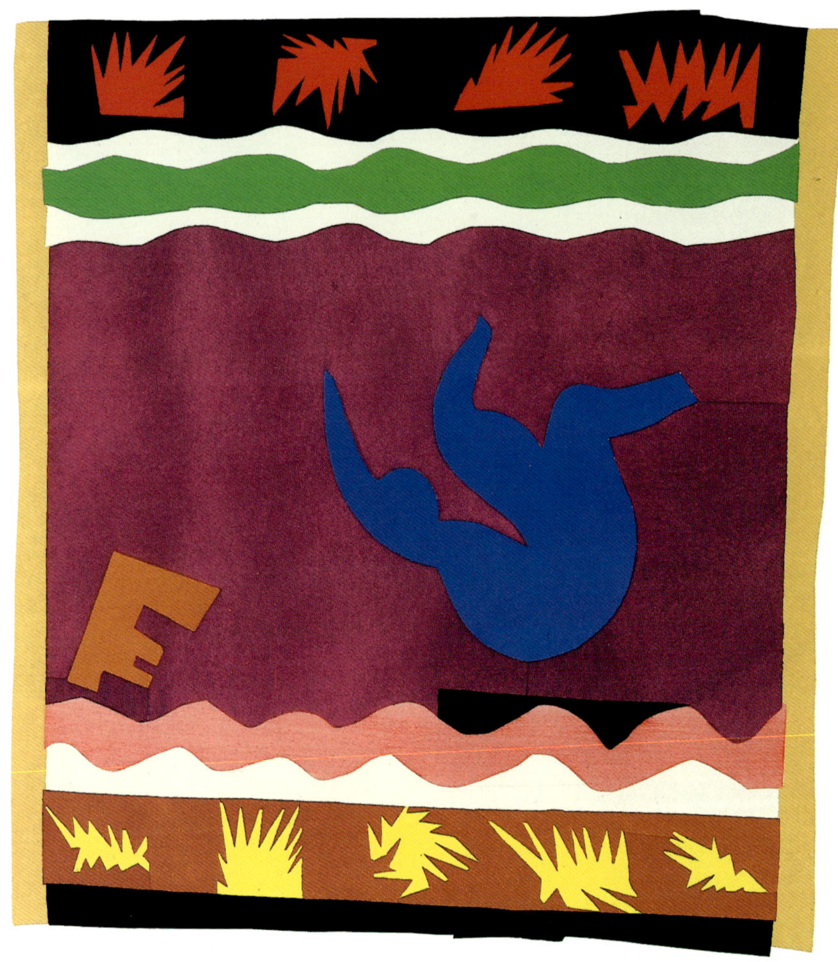

…I tend toward what I feel; toward a kind of ecstasy.
And then I find tranquility.

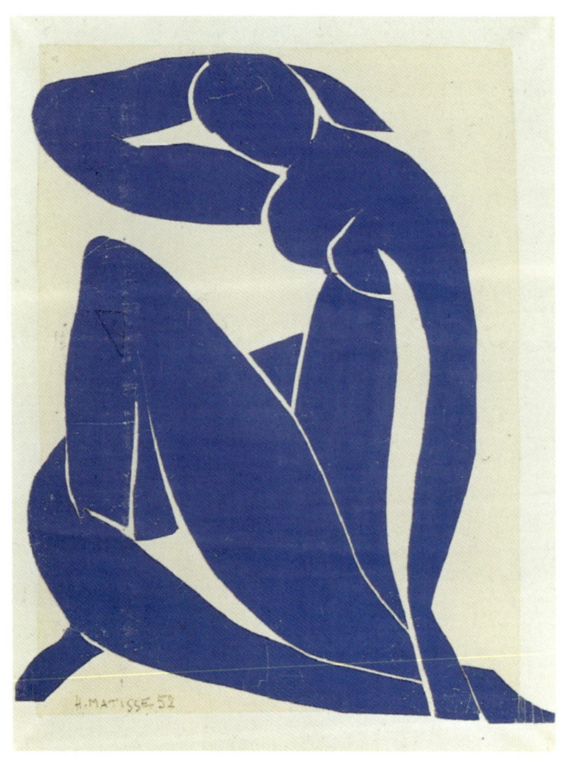
H. MATISSE 52

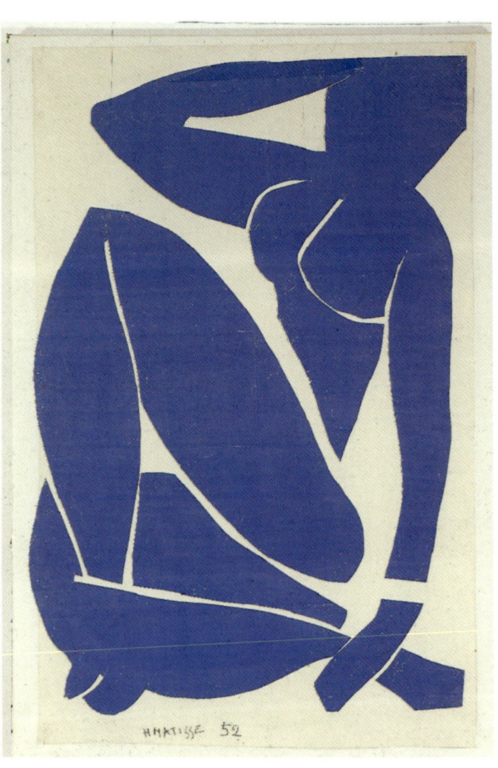
H MATISSE 52

If in the picture there is order and clarity it means that this same order and clarity existed in the mind of the painter and that the painter was conscious of their necessity. Limbs may cross, may mingle, but still in the eyes of the beholder they will remain attached to the right body. All confusion will have disappeared.

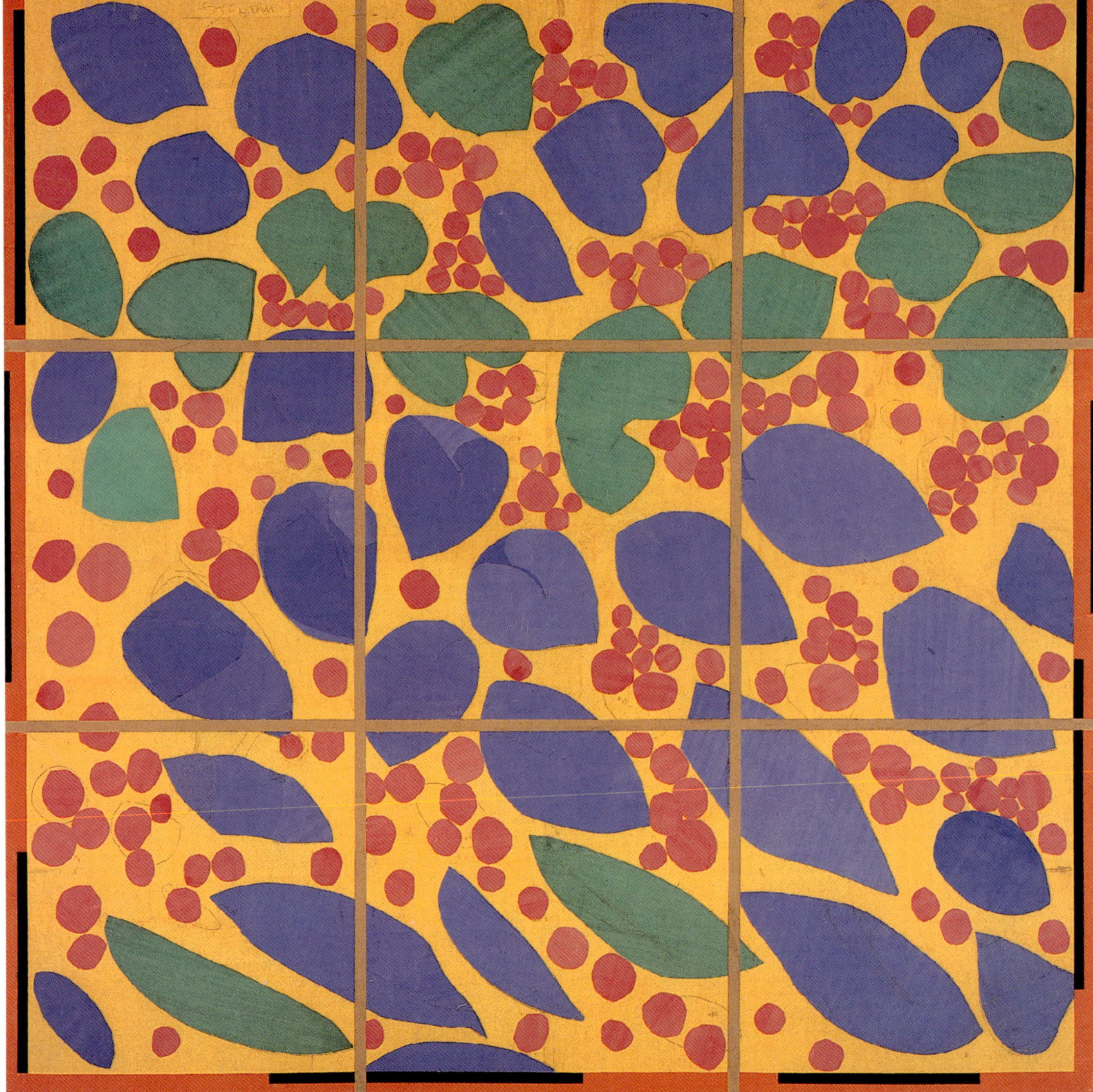

I feel very strongly the bond between my old works and my recent ones. But I do not think the way I thought yesterday. My fundamental thoughts have not changed but have evolved and my modes of expression have followed my thoughts. I do not repudiate any of my paintings, but I would not paint one of them in the same way had I to do it again. My destination is always the same but I work out a different route to get there.

So I have been no more than a medium, as it were.

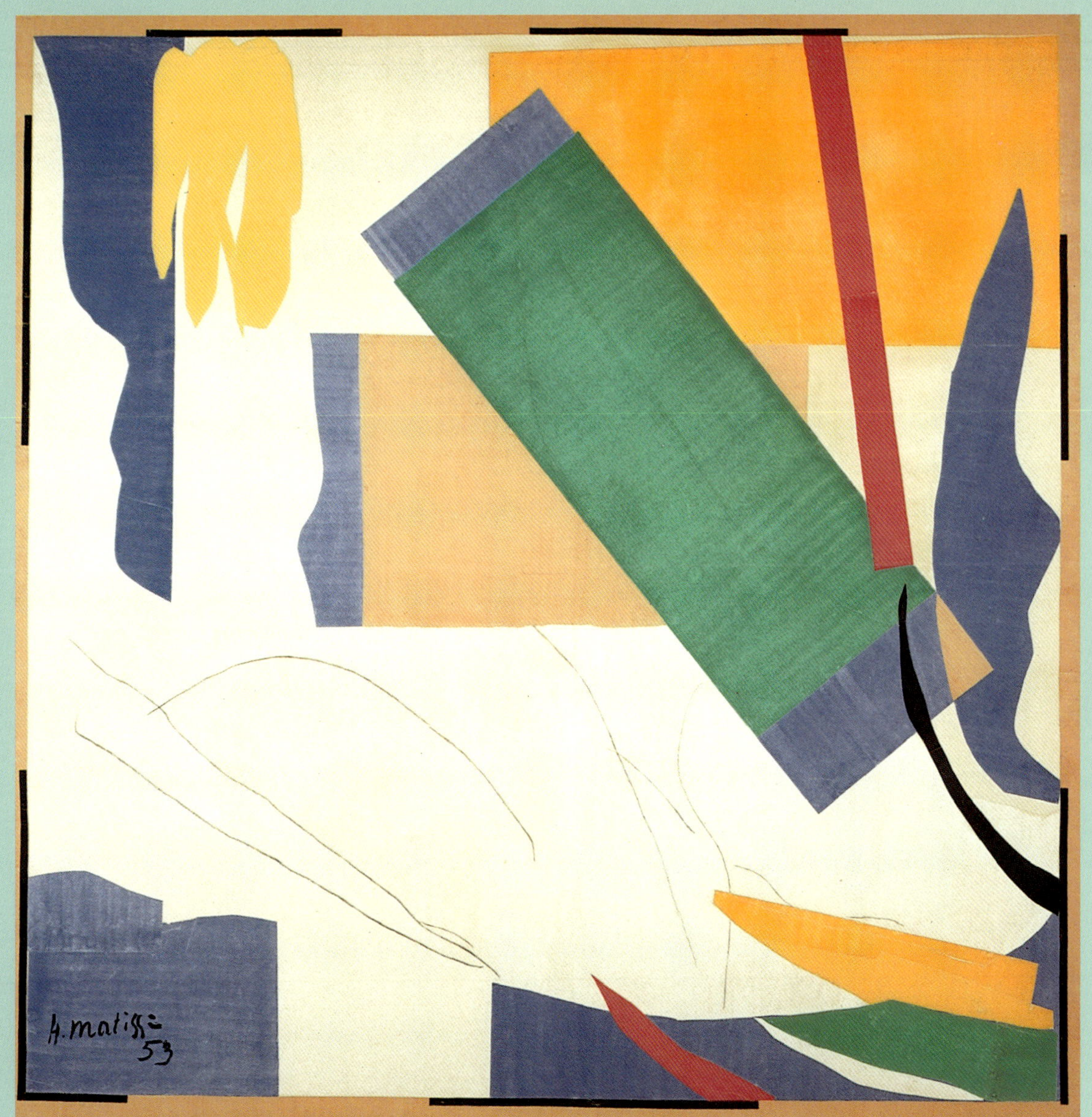
H. matisse
53

NOTES

1 Matisse wrote this as an adult to describe his early and unique fascination with painting. A sickly child (he was diagnosed with chronic appendicitis), Matisse was encouraged to take up less active hobbies. Who could have guessed where it would lead? No date. Quoted in *Matisse: The Man and His Art, 1869-1918.* Jack Flam. (Ithaca, NY: Cornell University Press). Copyright 1986.

5 From one of two radio interviews Matisse gave in 1942. Reprinted in *Matisse: His Art and His Public.* Alfred H. Barr, Jr. (New York: The Museum of Modern Art). Copyright 1951.

5 From the introduction to *Jazz,* an exultant collection of images and writing by Matisse, originally published by Matisse's publisher and colleague Teríade in 1946. Matisse created the images in *Jazz* inspired by "the circus, folktales, and voyages." English translation by Sophie Hawkes. (New York: George Braziller). Copyright 1985. Estate of Henri Matisse.

5 Description by longtime friend, admirer, and artist Françoise Gilot in her book *Matisse and Picasso: A Friendship in Art.* (New York: Doubleday). Copyright 1990.

6 A common statement by Picasso recorded by Gilot in *Matisse and Picasso: A Friendship in Art.*

9 No date. Remark repeated in Maurice Raynal et al, *History of Modern Painting: Matisse, Munch, Roualt—Fauvism, Expressionism.* (Geneva: Skira). Copyright 1950. Reprinted in *Henri Matisse: A Retrospective.* John Elderfield. (New York: Museum of Modern Art). Copyright 1992.

11 From *Notes d'un Peintre,* Henri Matisse's definitive early work. Originally published on December 25, 1908, in *La Grande Revue* in Paris, *Notes d'un Peintre* was a response to his critics. English version translated by Margaret Scolari and printed in 1931 by The Museum of Modern Art. Reprinted in its entirety in *Matisse: His Art and His Public.* Alfred H. Barr, Jr. (New York: The Museum of Modern Art). Copyright 1951.

13 Matisse, later in life, describing the Fauves (meaning "savages") at the height of their experimentation with color and composition. No date. The 1905 Salon d'Automne was the first noted exhibition of Fauvist work which took the Parisian art world by storm. Originally quoted in Gaston Diehl's biography of Matisse, *Henri Matisse* (Paris: Pierre Tisné, 1954), and reprinted in *Henri Matisse: A Retrospective.*

14 A remark recorded in the interview "Matisse Speaks" in 1951. Reprinted in *Matisse: The Man and His Art, 1869-1918.*

17 Statement made to close friend and biographer Louis Aragon. Printed in Aragon's *Henri Matisse: A Novel.* Vol 1. (London: Collins). Copyright 1972 and reprinted in *Henri Matisse: A Retrospective.* Matisse would often say that he painted signs and symbols, not objects.

19 1908, from *Notes d'un Peintre.*

20 Matisse speaking to his students in 1908. Sarah Stein, sister of Gertrude, was a loyal friend and student of Matisse at the Academie Matisse. There she took extensive notes. Reprinted in their entirety in *Matisse: His Art and His Public.* Alfred H. Barr, Jr. (New York: The Museum of Modern Art). Copyright 1951.

23 Commonly quoted passage from Matisse in the interview "Henri Matisse" with writer and supporter Guillaume Apollinaire in 1907.

24 1908, Matisse speaking to his students. Notes from Sarah Stein. Reprinted in *Matisse: His Art and His Public.*

27 Ibid.

28 Ibid.

31 Ibid.

33 From *Jazz,* 1946.

35 Remark describing the creation of his masterpiece *Dance*, 1910. Matisse first drew the images and then filled them in with color. Reprinted in *Henri Matisse: A Retrospective.*

37 From "L'exactitude n'est pas la Verité," an essay written by Matisse for inclusion in the Philadelphia Museum of Art Catalog in 1947. Translated by Esther Rowland Clifford. Reprinted in its entirety in *Henri Matisse: His Art and His Public.*

39 1908, from *Notes d'un Peintre.*

40 Originally quoted in Jacques Guenne, "Entretien avec Henri Matisse in L'art Vivant," Vol.1, No. 18. (September 15, 1925). Translated by Jack Flam, copyright 1973. Reprinted in *Henri Matisse: A Retrospective.*

43 No date. From a conversation with Picasso about why Matisse loved to paint interiors. Recorded by Gilot in *Matisse and Picasso: A Friendship in Art.*

44 1946, from *Jazz.*

47 Remark made by Matisse in a 1929 interview. Quoted in *Matisse: The Man and His Art, 1869-1918.*

48 Matisse speaking about his *Themes* and *Variations* drawings, no date. Quoted in Louis Aragon's *Henri Matisse: A Novel* (1972) and reprinted in *Matisse: The Wonder of Color.*

51 1908, from *Notes d'un Peintre.*

52 Famous quote from *Notes d'un Peintre,* 1908.

54 Letter from Henri Matisse while in Nice to his son Pierre in 1940. Reprinted in its entirety in *Matisse: His Art and His Public.*

57 Matisse speaking to Teríade as to why he journeyed to Tahiti in 1939. Printed in *Matisse: In the Collection of The Museum of Modern Art.* John Elderfield. (New York: The Museum of Modern Art). Copyright 1978.

58 Matisse speaking to his students, 1908. Notes from Sarah Stein.

61 A remark to writer and biographer Pierre Courthion in 1931 about the inability of the artist to see the meaning in his own work. Reprinted in *Henri Matisse: A Retrospective.*

63 1908, from *Notes d'un Peintre.*

65 Ibid.

66 Appears in *Matisse on Art* by Jack Flam (1973). Reprinted in *Henri Matisse: A Retrospective.*

68 1908, from *Notes d'un Peintre.*

70 Ibid.

72 From a letter written on June 1, 1916, to friend and student Hans Purrmann. Matisse was painting at Issy during this part of World War I. Printed in its entirety in *Matisse: His Art and His Public.*

75 1947, from "L'exactitude n'est pas la Verité." Translated by Esther Rowland Clifford. Reprinted in its entirety in *Henri Matisse: His Art and His Public.*

77 1907 statement to Hans Purrmann. Quoted in *Matisse: The Man and His Art, 1869-1918.*

79 1908, from *Notes d'un Peintre.*

80 Ibid.

82 Ibid.

85 A statement made in 1913 to Marcel Sembat, who had just seen *The Moorish Café* hanging at a show. Reprinted in *Matisse: His Art and His Public.*

87 1908, from *Notes d'un Peintre.*

89 Ibid.

90 Part of Matisse's 1952 inauguration address "Message à sa ville natale" at the opening of the Musee Matisse in his hometown, Le Cateau-Cambrésis. Translated by Pierre Schneider in his book, *Matisse* (New York: Rizzoli). Copyright 1984.

96 1908, from *Notes d'un Peintre.*

LIST OF PLATES

1 *Auto-portrait (Self-portrait),* 1918/Oil on canvas/Collection Musée Matisse, Le Cateau-Cambrésis

2 *Interior with Dog,* 1934/Oil on canvas/The Baltimore Museum of Art/The Cone Collection, formed by Dr. Claribel Cone and Miss Etta Cone of Baltimore, Maryland, BMA 1950.257

7 *La Fille aux Yeux Verts (The Girl with Green Eyes),* 1908/Oil on canvas, 26" x 20"/San Francisco Museum of Modern Art/Bequest of Harriet Lane Levy

8 *Woman Reading (La Liseuse),* 1895/Musée National d'Art Moderne/Centre National d'Art et de Culture Georges Pompidou, Paris, France

9 *Studio under the Eaves (L'atelier sous les toits),* 1901-2/Oil on canvas/Fitzwilliam Museum, Cambridge, England/Photograph © 1995 Fitzwilliam Museum, University of Cambridge

10 *A Glimpse of Notre Dame in the Late Afternoon,* 1902/Oil on paper mounted on canvas, 28 1/2" x 21 1/2"/Albright-Knox Art Gallery, Buffalo, New York/Gift of Seymour H. Knox, 1927

12 *Luxe, Calme, et Volupté,* 1904-5/Oil on canvas/Musée d'Orsay, Paris/Photograph © 1996 R.M.N.

15 *Nude in the Wood,* 1905/Oil on canvas/The Brooklyn Museum, 52.150/Gift of Mr. George F. Of

16 *Self-portrait,* 1906/Oil on canvas/Statens-Museum for Kunst, Soelvgade, Copenhagen/Photo: Hans Petersen

17 Detail from *Harbor at Collioure (Port de Collioure),* 1907/Lithograph, printed in black, composition: 4 5/16" x 7 5/8"/The Museum of Modern Art, New York/Given in memory of Leo and Nina Stein/Photograph © 1996 The Museum of Modern Art, New York

18 *Marine (Bord de Mer) [Seascape (Beside the Sea)],* 1905-6/Oil on cardboard mounted on panel, 9 5/8" x 12 3/4"/San Francisco Museum of Modern Art/Bequest of Mildred B. Bliss

18 *Marine (La Moulade) (Seascape),* ca. 1905-6/Oil on cardboard mounted on panel, 10 1/4" x 13 1/4"/San Francisco Museum of Modern Art/Bequest of Mildred B. Bliss

19 *Paysage: Les Genets (The Broom Trees),* 1905/Oil on panel, 12" x 15 5/8"/San Francisco Museum of Modern Art/Bequest of Elise S. Haas

21 *Seated Nude (Nu Assis) (Petit Bois Clair),* Paris, early 1906/Woodcut, printed in black, composition: 13 7/16" x 10 7/16"/The Museum of Modern Art, New York/Abby Aldrich Rockefeller Fund

22 *The Geranium,* 1906/Oil on canvas, 101.3 cm x 82.6 cm/Joseph Winterbotham Collection, 1932.1342/Photograph © 1995 The Art Institute of Chicago, All Rights Reserved

25 *Brook with Aloes,* 1907/Oil on canvas, 23 3/4" x 23 5/8" /The Menil Collection, Houston/Photo: Hickey-Robertson, Houston

26 *Femme au Chapeau (Woman with Hat),* 1905/Oil on canvas, 31 3/4" x 23 1/2"/San Francisco Museum of Modern Art/Elise S. Haas Collection

29 *Breakfast,* 1921/Oil on canvas/The Philadelphia Museum of Art/The Samuel S. White 3rd and Vera White Collection

30 *Bathers with a Turtle,* 1908/Oil on canvas/The Saint Louis Art Museum/Gift of Mr. and Mrs. Joseph Pulitzer, Jr.

32 *Nasturtiums and the "Dance" (II),* 1912/Oil on canvas/The Metropolitan Museum of Art/Bequest of Scofield Thayer, 1982 (1984.433.16)/Photograph © 1994 The Metropolitan Museum of Art

34-35 *Dance (First Version),* Paris, March, 1909/Oil on canvas, 8' 6 1/2" x 12' 9 1/2"/The Museum of Modern Art, New York/Photograph © 1995 The Museum of Modern Art, New York

36 *Algerian Woman (L'Algerienne),* 1909/Musée National d'Art Moderne/Centre National d'Art et de Culture Georges Pompidou, Paris, France

38 *Pianist and Checker Players,* 1924/Oil on canvas/Collection of Mr. and Mrs. Paul Mellon/© 1995 Board of Trustees, National Gallery of Art, Washington

41 *Moroccan Garden,* Tangier, 1912/Oil, pencil, and charcoal on canvas, 46" x 32 1/4"/The Museum of Modern Art, New York/Gift of Florence M. Schoenborn/Photograph © 1996 The Museum of Modern Art, New York

42 *The Red Studio,* Issy-les-Moulineaux, 1911/Oil on canvas, 71 1/4" x 7' 2 1/4"/The Museum of Modern Art, New York /Mrs. Simon Guggenheim Fund/Photograph © 1995 The Museum of Modern Art, New York

45 *A Basket of Oranges (Corbeille d'Oranges),* 1912/Oil on canvas/Musée Picasso, Paris/Photograph © 1996 R.M.N.

46 *The Blue Window,* Issy-les-Moulineaux, summer 1913/Oil on canvas, 51 1/2" x 35 5/8"/The Museum of Modern Art, New York/Abby Aldrich Rockefeller Fund/Photograph © 1996 The Museum of Modern Art, New York

49 *Three-Quarter Nude, Head Partly Showing (Nude trois-quarts, une*

partie de la tête coupée), 1913/Transfer lithograph, printed in black, composition: 19 13/16" x 12"/The Museum of Modern Art, New York/Frank Crowninshield Fund/Photograph © 1996 The Museum of Modern Art, New York

50 *French Window at Collioure (Porte-Fenetre a Collioure),* 1914/Musée National d'Art Moderne/Centre National d'Art et de Culture Georges Pompidou, Paris, France

53 *Artist and Goldfish,* Paris, winter 1914/Oil on canvas, 57 3/4" x 44 1/4"/The Museum of Modern Art, New York/Gift of Florence M. Schoenborn and Samuel A. Marx (the former retaining a life interest)/Photograph © 1995 The Museum of Modern Art, New York

55 *Anemones in an Earthenware Vase (Les Anémones),* 1924/Oil on canvas/Kunstmuseum, Bern, Switzerland/Photograph © VAGA, New York

56 *Piano Lesson,* Issy-les-Moulineaux, late summer 1916/Oil on canvas, 8' 1/2" x 6' 11 3/4"/The Museum of Modern Art, New York/Gift of Mrs. Simon Guggenheim Fund/Photograph © 1996 The Museum of Modern Art, New York

58 *Study for Portrait of Sarah Stein,* 1916/Graphite on paper, 19 1/8" x 12 5/8"/San Francisco Museum of Modern Art/Gift of Mr. and Mrs. Walter A. Haas

59 *Portrait of Sarah Stein,* 1916/Oil on board, 28 1/2" x 22 1/4"/San Francisco Museum of Modern Art /Sarah and Michael Stein Memorial Collection, Gift of Elise Stern Haas

60 *Interior with a Violin Case,* Nice, winter 1918-19/Oil on canvas, 28 3/4" x 23 5/8"/The Museum of Modern Art, New York/Lillie P. Bliss Collection/Photograph © 1996 The Museum of Modern Art, New York

61 *Interior with a Violin,* 1918/Oil on canvas/Statens-Museum for Kunst, Soelvgade, Copenhagen

62 *Interior in Yellow & Blue (Interieur en jaune et bleu),* 1946/Musée National d'Art Moderne/Centre National d'Art et de Culture Georges Pompidou, Paris, France

63 *Still Life with Lemons*/Oil on canvas/Courtesy, Museum of Art, Rhode Island School of Design/Gift of Miss Edith Wetmore/Photography by Cathy Carver

64 *Tea,* 1919/Oil on canvas/Los Angeles County Museum of Art/Bequest of David L. Loew in memory of his father, Marcus Loew

67 *White Plumes,* 1919/Oil on canvas/The Minneapolis Institute of Arts/The William Hood Dunwoody Fund

69 *Reclining Nude,* 1927/Pen and ink, 10 7/8" x 15"/The Museum of Modern Art, New York/The Tisch Foundation, Inc. Fund/Photograph © 1996 The Museum of Modern Art, New York

70-71 *Large Reclining Nude, formerly The Pink Nude,* 1935/Oil on canvas/The Baltimore Museum of Art/The Cone Collection, formed by Dr. Claribel Cone and Miss Etta Cone of Baltimore, Maryland, BMA 1950.258

73 *Woman in a Purple Coat,* 1937/Oil on canvas/The Museum of Fine Arts, Houston/The John A. and Audrey Jones Beck Collection

74 (also back cover) *Self-portrait,* 1937/Charcoal and estompe/The Baltimore Museum of Art/The Cone Collection, formed by Dr. Claribel Cone and Miss Etta Cone of Baltimore, Maryland, BMA 1950.12.61

76 *Still Life with Sleeping Woman,* 1940/Canvas/Oil on canvas/Collection of Mr. and Mrs. Paul Mellon/© 1995 Board of Trustees, National Gallery of Art, Washington

78 *The Romanian Blouse (La Blouse Roumaine),* 1940/Musée National d'Art Moderne/Centre National d'Art et de Culture Georges Pompidou, Paris, France

81 *The Rocaille Armchair (Fauteuil Rocaille),* Venice, 1946/Oil on canvas/Musée Matisse, Nice, France/Gift of Madame Henri Matisse, 1960

83 Detail from *Icarus,* plate VIII from *Jazz,* by Henri Matisse. Published Paris, E. Tériade, 1947/Pochoir, printed in color, each double page, 16 5/8" x 25 5/8"/The Museum of Modern Art, New York /The Louis E. Stern Collection/Photograph © 1996 The Museum of Modern Art, New York

84 (also cover) Detail from *Toboggan,* plate XX from *Jazz,* by Henri Matisse/Published Paris, E. Tériade, 1947/Pochoir, printed in color, double sheet 16 5/8" x 25 5/8"/The Museum of Modern Art, New York/The Louis E. Stern Collection/Photograph © 1996 The Museum of Modern Art, New York

86 *Blue Nude II and III (Nu Bleu II et III),* 1952/Musée National d'Art Moderne/Centre National d'Art et de Culture Georges Pompidou, Paris, France

88 *Ivy in Flower,* 1953/Colored paper and pencil 112" x 112", 1963.68 FA/Dallas Museum of Art, Foundation for the Arts Collection/Gift of the Albert and Mary Lasker Foundation/Photograph © 1992 Dallas Museum of Art, All Rights Reserved

91 *Memory of Oceania (Souvenir d'Océanie),* Nice, summer 1952-early 1953/Gouache and crayon on cut-and-pasted paper over canvas/9' 4" x 9' 4 7/8"/The Museum of Modern Art, New York/Mrs. Simon Guggenheim Fund/Photograph © 1996 The Museum of Modern Art, New York

All artists bear the imprint of their time
but the great artists are those in which this stamp
is most deeply impressed.